CENSORSHIP
500 YEARS OF CONFLICT

Humbly dedicated to the Jacobine Clubs of France & England! By Common Sense.

"These are your Gods, O, Israel!"

"Fathom & a half! Fathom & a half! Poor Tom!" ah! mercy upon me! that's more by half than my poor Measure will ever be able to reach! — Lord! Lord! I wish I had a bit of the Stay-tape or Buckram which I youst to Cabbage when I was prentice, to lengthen it out; — well, well, who could ever have thought it, that I, who have served Seven Years as an Apprentice, & afterwards worked Four Years as a Journeyman to a Master Taylor, then followd the business of an Exciseman as much longer, should not be able to take the dimensions of this Bauble! for what is a Crown but a Bauble! which we may see in the Tower for Six-pence a piece? — well, altho' it may be too large for a Taylor to take Measure of, there's one Comfort, he may make mouths at it & call it as many names as he pleases! — and yet, Lord, Lord, I should like to make it a Yankee-doodle Night Cap & Breeches, if it was not not so damn'd large, or I had stuff enough Ah! if I could once do that, I would soon stitch up the mouth of that Barnacled Edmund from making of any more Reflections upon the Flints — & so Flints & Liberty for ever — & damn the Dungs!!!

Pubd May 23th 1791. by H.Humphrey No.18,Old Bond Street

"THE RIGHTS OF MAN; — or TOMMY PAINE, the little American Taylor, taking the Measure of the CROWN, for a new Pair of Revolution Breeches.

CENSORSHIP

500 YEARS OF CONFLICT

The New York Public Library

NEW YORK   OXFORD

OXFORD UNIVERSITY PRESS

1984

Published for the exhibition *Censorship: 500 Years of Conflict,* The New York Public Library June 1—October 15, 1984.

This exhibition has been made possible by grants from the National Endowment for the Humanities, Washington, D.C., a Federal agency; The New York Times Company Foundation, Inc., Time Incorporated, Philip L. Graham Fund, and the New York State Council on the Arts, and by a general underwriting grant from Exxon Corporation.

This publication has been made possible by grants from The J. M. Kaplan Fund, Inc., and the National Endowment for the Humanities, Washington, D.C., a Federal agency.

Published by Oxford University Press, New York, in association with The New York Public Library, Fifth Avenue and 42nd Street, New York, N.Y. 10018. Printed in the U.S.A.

This publication was produced under the direction of Editors & Scholars, a nonprofit service of The Institute for Research in History.

EDITOR:	William Zeisel
DESIGNER:	Brian Rushton
PHOTOGRAPHERS:	*(front cover)* Paul Warchol
	(text illustrations) Robert D. Rubic
TYPESETTING:	American TypeCrafters, Inc., New York
PRINTING:	Conceptual Litho Reproductions, Inc., New York

First edition set in Trump Medieval; text printed on Warren Cameo Dull 80lb; endpapers on Lindenmeyr Multicolor® Antique Thistle.

Front cover:
Freedom in Flames. Photograph © Paul Warchol, 1984. Commissioned by The New York Public Library on the occasion of the exhibition *Censorship: 500 Years of Conflict.* [On July 4, 1854, the abolitionist leader William Lloyd Garrison publicly burned a copy of the United States Constitution in Framingham, Massachusetts. This symbolic protest rested on Garrison's belief that the Constitution protected slavery in the Southern states.]

Endpapers:
Jean-Ignace Isidor Gérard, called Grandville, **The Descent on the Pressroom of Liberty of the Press.** From *L'Association mensuelle,* November 1833. *Courtesy Jane Voorhees Zimmerli Art Museum, Rutgers the State University of New Jersey;* "Friends" purchase.

Frontispiece:
James Gillray, **The Rights of Man.** 1791. When Tom Paine was convicted of seditious libel for attacking the monarchy in his book, *The Second Part of the Rights of Man,* he fled to France. This satirical print shows him taking measurements for an English revolution. *Ex. no. 147*

Library of Congress Cataloging in Publication Data

Main entry under title
Censorship: 500 years of conflict.

    1. Censorship—History—Exhibitions. 2. Freedom of the press—History—Exhibitions. 3. Condemned books—Exhibitions 4. Prohibited books—Exhibitions. 5. Bibliographical exhibitions—New York (N.Y.) I. New York Public Library.
Z657.C4 1984   098'.12'07401471   84-8320
ISBN 0-19-503529-1
ISBN 0-87104-284-3 (pbk.)

▲   Hans Sebald Beham. **Biblische Historien figürlich fürbildet.** 1536. *Ex. no. 12*

Preface

ARTHUR SCHLESINGER, JR.

Censorship has of course been around for a good deal longer than the five centuries covered in this exhibition. "Tell it not in Gath," the Old Testament reminds us, "publish it not in the streets of Askelon; lest the daughters of the Philistines rejoice, lest the daughters of the uncircumcised triumph." Greek philosophers agreed in proclaiming the virtues of suppression. "The poet," wrote Plato, "shall compose nothing contrary to the ideas of the lawful, or just, or beautiful, or good, which are allowed in the state; nor shall he be permitted to show his compositions to any private individual, until he shall have shown them to the appointed censors and the guardians of the law, and they are satisfied with them."

Through most of human history, authority, thus fortified by the highest religious and philosophical texts, has righteously invoked censorship to stifle expression. The significance of the New York Public Library's *500 Years of Conflict* is that these are the years which witnessed the great shift in the moral balance between expression and authority. In earlier times only heretics and blasphemers had dared challenge traditional claims of authority over expression. The last five centuries have finally established powerful claims of expression against authority.

The emancipation of expression has been slow, painful, and incomplete. Even today the benefits are mostly confined to the small minority of nations practicing self-government and civic freedom. Tyranny still crushes expression in vast stretches of the contemporary world. Nevertheless, the principle of free expression has at last achieved moral status and in 1948 was solemnly enshrined in the United Nations Universal Declaration of Human Rights. If this document has thus far had the most meager impact on actual conditions, the standards it declares will guide the struggle in the years to come.

As the following essays richly show, a variety of developments combined to strengthen expression in the battle against authority. Technological change, especially the invention of the printing press, economic change, especially the emergence of the middle class, political change, especially the rise of democracy, and philosophical change, especially the spread of science and secularization—all united to diversify the social order and to accord new rights to expression. Individuals and groups were prepared to concede liberty of expression to others in order to assure it for themselves; and censorship, except at the margins, began to lose legitimacy. Once liberty was perceived as a practical necessity, John Stuart Mill was able to transform it into a supreme ethical principle.

But the struggle between expression and authority is unending. The instinct to suppress discomforting ideas is rooted deep in human nature. It is rooted above all in profound human propensities to faith and to fear.

The true believer is always an incipient censor. People who are absolutely certain where truth lies feel morally justified in suppressing heresy, lest the daughters of the Philistines rejoice and the daughters of the uncircumcised triumph. Burning at the stake is the way to save a sinner's soul. "A fanatic," said Mr. Dooley, "is a man that does what he thinks th' Lord wud do if He knew th' facts iv th' case." The old supernatural religions bred fanaticism. So today do the new social religions of the totalitarian states. Absolutists, whether religious or secular, cannot bear to acknowledge their own fallibility. They cannot bring themselves to say with Mill, "We can never be sure that the opinion we are endeavouring to stifle is a false opinion; and if we were sure, stifling it would be an evil still."

ARTHUR SCHLESINGER, JR. is Schweitzer Professor of the Humanities at the Graduate School, The City University of New York. A Pulitzer Prize winner in both history and biography, he has written widely on American culture and politics. His many books include *A Thousand Days* (Boston: Houghton Mifflin, 1965) and *The Imperial Presidency* (Boston: Houghton Mifflin, 1973). From 1961 to 1964 Professor Schlesinger was Special Assistant to the President of the United States.

משום מתנה אלא היכא שמן המכס עושין תשמישי
עבודה [redacted] · ויש מקומות שנוהגין עבודה [redacted]
וקבלו עליהם הסוחרים שבכל דבר שימכרו שיתנו
פשוט ל[redacted] לבניי׳ לשם כר׳ שאם אמ׳ לישרא׳ קח החפץ
בכך ועוד פשוט לבניין עבודה [redacted] לשם אמרינן
דמתנה אסור ואם אינו מזכיר לו פשוט לבניי׳ עבודה
[redacted] מות׳ אף על גב דה[redacted] יתן לו מדמי׳ של מקח זה
דשמא בלא זה לא היה נותן לו החפץ כי אם בדמים
הללו ואם יותר מן המכס אמר לו ועוד פשוט אף על
גב שלא הזכיר לו לצורך עבודה [redacted] שהניח לומר
כן בשביל הישרא׳ שמא אסור דהשת׳ יוצא מכיסו של
ישרא׳ הפשוט דאי לאו הבניי׳ הוה מחיל ליה לגביה ׃

קלח אילו דברים שאין מ
מוכרי׳ להם ל[redacted]

איסטרובלין ולבונה כו׳ ושאר דברים שתמן מותר
ופירושן אסור אם כן [redacted] שעובר משום לפני עור · וכן שעוה ביום
[redacted] שלהן [redacted] למכור לשוש[redacted] שעושי׳ ממנה
תקרובת ועובר משום לפני עור אבל בשאר יומי
מותר למכור להן שעוה וכן [redacted] שישראל קונה
לאחר שפגמו [redacted] אסור למוכרן ל[redacted] דבשביל פגימ׳
קטנה אין מניח [redacted] לתת בה יין לקלס עבודה [redacted]
שלו וכן [redacted] אסור למכור להן ועובר משום
לפני עור וכן נמי אמרינ׳ פרק קונם רב אשי הוה ליה
תכא זבניה לבי נורא ל[redacted] שמה כך א״ל רבינ׳ והא
עבר לפני עור אמר ליה סתם עצים להסקה ניתנו
ולא לשרוף תקרובת הא לאו הכי אסו׳ וכן פירש הר״ר
אליעזר ברבי שמואל ממיץ בפירוש נדרים ׃

קלט אין מקדישין בזמן הזה ואם
הקדיש כסות וכלי׳ ופירות
ירקבו מעות וכלי מתכות יוליכם לים המלח בהמה
תעקר ואיזהו עיקור נועל דלת בפניה ומתה מאליה
אם כן אסור בזמן הזה להקדיש אבל יאמ׳ אני נותן
חפץ זה או דמיו לצדקה לעניים או למצוה זו ׃

אין מוכרין להם בהמה גסה עגלים
וסייחים שלמים ושבורים ר׳ יהודה
מתיר בשבורה בן בתירה מתיר בסוס וטעמא דאין
מוכרין גזירה משום שאלה ושכירות ועובר משום ל
למען ינוח שורך דאגרא לא קני׳ אף על גב דבפרק
הזהב אמרינן דאונאה שייך בשכירו׳ דמי כתיב וכי
תמכרו ממכר לעולם ממכר בן יומו קרוי ממכר ואף
על גב דקרוי מכר מכל מקו׳ אינו קרוי בהמתו וביתו

של מוכר כי אם של משכיר וגם טעמא דאין מוכרין
להם בהמ׳ גסה משו׳ כשיוני דזמנין דסמוך לשקיעת
החמה דמעלי שבתא א״ל ישראל ל[redacted] כשייה ושמעה
קליה דישראל ואזלא מחמתיה ועובר משום מחמר
אחר בהמתו בשבת ואסור משו׳ לא תעש׳ כל מלאכה
פ׳ מי שהחשיך אבל לא רצה לומר טעמ׳ דלמען ינוח
שורך דשמא משום גזירת איסור בהמתו שאין תלוי
בגופו לא היו אוסרין למכור ל[redacted] רבא שרא לזבוני
חמרא לגוי אידיא דספסיר׳ אי משום כשיוני לא ידעא
ליה לקליה · אי משו׳ שאלה ושכירות כיון דלאו דידיה
הוא לא מושיל ולא מוגיר ועוד משו׳ דלא מגלי מומא
רב הונא זבין ההיא פרה לגוי אמר ליה רב מאי ט
טעמא עבד מר הכי אמר ליה אימר לשחיטה זבנה
ומתניתין דקתני דאין מוכרין להן בהמה גסה וכו׳
מיירי שפיר שא״ל ה[redacted] למלאכה אני צריך לה ובהמה
טמאה אפילו בסתמא אסור דהא לאו לאכילה קיימא
כך פירש ר״שי מ״כ · ורבינו שמואל מ״כ פירש דפרה
נקבה לאו בת מלאכה היא כל כך ומתניתין דאסרה
בשור זכר כדאמרן פ׳ המוכר פירות גבי שור ונמצא
נגחן רובא לרדיא זבני ולקמן גבי שור של פטם כי
משהי ליה עד שתכחש אתי לכלל מלאכה ובהמה
גסה דמתניתא מיירי בבהמה טמאה כגון סוסים
וחמורים דבני מלאכה נינהו ורבינו תם מפר׳ דפרה
נמי נקבה בת מלאכה היא כדאמרינן כהן שמכר
פרה מישר׳ וכן לא ימכור לו פרה החורשת בשביע׳
וכן פרק קמא דפסחים שתי פרות החורשות בהר
המשח׳ וכן השואל את הפרה שאל אחת ושכר אחת
לכך מפרש דבין זכר ובין נקבה איכא למימר אימר
לשחיטה זבנה ומותר למכור [redacted] ובהמ׳ גסה דאסר
מתניתין בהמה טמאה כגון סוסים וחמורים אבל
בהמ׳ טהורה לא ומתני׳ אסרה דווקא עגלים וסייחי׳
קטנים שדרכן לגדל ומסתמא אין רגילות לקנותן
לגדל כדי לשחטן כי אם למלאכה ולקמן דקאמ׳ גבי
שור של פטם דאימר אסור דלשחיטה קא בעי לה ·
יש לומר כיון דאמר לקמן בדתורי משהי׳ להו ועביד
מלאכה על חד תרין איכא למימר דקונהו למלאכה
לאחר שיהא כחוש · מיהו רבינו תם מפרש שאינו
מפוטם עדיין אלא קונהו לפטם וכיון שמשהא אותו
לפטם יש לחוש יותר מבסתם פרה או שור דכיון ד
דמשהא לה לפיטום ולשחוט מימליך ומשהי ליה נמי
לעשות בו מלאכה ושבור׳ דאסרי לה רבנן דר׳ יהוד׳
לכל הפחות בעגלי׳ וסייחי׳ היינו טעמא כיון דמשהי
ליה

Censorship springs too from fear. Novelty is inherently disruptive and subversive. Nothing is more threatening than the promise to upset the settled order of understanding. "The key to all ages," said Emerson, "is—Imbecility in the vast majority of men, at all times, and, even in heroes, in all but certain eminent moments, victims of gravity, custom, and fear." People act to protect themselves against expression that, by articulating repressed urges or by affirming new ideas or values, incites doubt, disturbance, disorder.

So censorship remains a lurking possibility in the freest of societies. And even the libertarian must reluctantly allow that there is a point at which liberty passes into license—as, for example, the sale of hardcore pornography to children. Mill himself defined a class of acts "which, being directly injurious only to the agents themselves, ought not to be legally interdicted, but which, if done publicly...and coming thus within the category of offences against others, may rightfully be prohibited. Of this kind are offences against decency."

Yet history shows repeatedly what folly is committed in the name of virtue. In March 1885 the board of trustees voted to exclude a book from the shelves of the Concord Public Library. The offending work, one trustee said, "deals with a series of adventures of a very low grade of morality; it is couched in the language of a rough dialect, and all through its pages there is a systematic use of bad grammar.... The book is flippant and irreverent.... It is trash of the veriest sort." This dangerous book was *The Adventures of Huckleberry Finn*. Before we laugh too easily at the panic of the Concord Public Library a century ago, let us reflect on what goes on in school libraries across the land of liberty now—the banning not only of pornography but of works by Bernard Malamud, Kurt Vonnegut, and other eminently serious writers. Even *Huck Finn* itself, a century later, is still in jeopardy; the reasons are different from those of 1885 but no more convincing. In too many American communities today, cultural vigilantism, organized by the fanatical and the fearful, is an active menace.

Yet in these five hundred years of conflict, suppression has lost its moral advantage, at least in democratic nations, and, in such nations, censorship generally rebounds against the censor. When Mark Twain heard what the Concord Public Library had done, he remarked, "That will sell 25,000 copies for us, sure." "Every burned book," said Emerson, "enlightens the world; every suppressed or expunged word reverberates through the earth." Emerson's dictum will be true, however, only when readers stand boldly against censors. As Elmer Davis said during the high noon of McCarthyism, "This will remain the land of the free only so long as it is the home of the brave."

As for those vast regions of the world sadly sunk in fanaticism and despotism, we fortunate ones on this side of the moon must forever celebrate those brave men and women, like A. D. Sakharov, who intrepidly and at awful risk affirm the rights of expression against the tyranny of authority.

HUCKLEBERRY FINN.

▲   Mark Twain, **Adventures of Huckleberry Finn.** 1885. *Ex. no. 185*

◄   Baruch ben Isaac, **Sefer ha-Terumah.** 1523. Shown is a portion of a code of Jewish law that discusses the prohibition of idolatry (lit. "strange worship"). Here the words for strange and Gentile have been crossed out, as well as longer passages, which the Catholic censors found objectionable. *Ex. no. 25*

Foreword

VARTAN GREGORIAN

VARTAN GREGORIAN is President and Chief Executive Officer of The New York Public Library.

Censorship: 500 Years of Conflict marks for the Library both an important rededication and a new beginning.

This major exhibition, the first undertaken by the Library in two generations, signals a recommitment to our historic role: the sharing of a vast body of thought preserved in the books, prints, and manuscripts that record our civilization, and which it is the Library's privilege and mission to preserve.

The restored main exhibition hall, which has been renamed the D. Samuel and Jeane H. Gottesman Exhibition Hall, will provide a continuing opportunity for scholars and the public at large to discover and rediscover our collection, which ranks among the greatest in the world, and many of whose treasures have until now been seen by few contemporary New Yorkers.

Censorship: 500 Years of Conflict also marks a new era of interpretative exhibitions at the Library, which will add an important dimension to public life in New York. With its four concomitant exhibitions at The Research Libraries, *Censorship: 500 Years of Conflict* is providing for the first time a broad city-wide context for citizens and visitors to participate in the understanding of one of the key issues of our age. The exhibitions will be elaborated through lectures, forums, films, and dialogues on the subject at neighborhoods that are served by The Branch Libraries throughout the city.

Although few believe an Orwellian world is here, many do recognize that freedom of expression is still facing serious challenges in our society. As a symbol of free and unfettered access to knowledge, the Library is the uniquely appropriate site for this important exhibition, and 1984 could not be a more apt time to reassess censorship, past and present, in Western culture.

Although the Library's collections are universal in scope and so rich that they could support exhibitions on censorship in almost any culture, language, historical period, or medium, this exhibition draws on the Library's extensive European and American holdings. The nearly 300 items, almost entirely from the Library's own holdings, feature books, manuscripts, and prints that illustrate significant struggles over freedom of expression from 1450 to the present. The four complementary exhibitions on particular aspects of censorship are based on other specialties of The Research Libraries' collections: *Censorship in the Slavic World; Censorship and Black America; Censorship and Libraries Today;* and *Censorship in British and American Theatre.* The series of public forums that the Library is sponsoring will feature prominent scholars and public figures discussing contemporary issues of censorship.

These exhibitions and programs all underscore the fact that censorship is a universal phenomenon. At any time, two fundamental and conflicting historical forces seem to be at work: one is demonstrated by such authors as Milton, Paine, and Orwell, who sought to protect the integrity of the printed word and the quest for free inquiry, while the opposing force is represented by the moral censors of the nineteenth century—and the state and church authorities of earlier periods. These sought to protect the stability of the traditional order from various challenges including those expressed in books, pamphlets, and printed images. Although the methods of censorship have changed, and the targets of the censor have shifted over the centuries, the tension between censor and critic remains constant in all organized society.

The visitor to *Censorship: 500 Years of Conflict* will find printed material of all kinds—the physical records that reflect this historic conflict. Here books and manuscripts, once the object of destruction, have been collected and preserved to be exhibited today. Materials once suppressed are now at the Library, free and accessible to any citizen who wishes to read and study them.

The Library could not have fulfilled its historic mission over the years without those who have contributed so much—the Astors, the Lenoxes, the

Tildens—as well as their twentieth-century successors and many major and minor collectors, donors, and benefactors.

We acknowledge the smallest contributor as well as the largest donor, and take this opportunity to extend our special appreciation to those who have made possible the restoration of the main exhibition hall: the D.S. and R.H. Gottesman Foundation; the Rockefeller Brothers Fund; the Uris Brothers Foundation, Inc.; and including such benefactors as Harold W. McGraw, Jr. and many other individuals whose contribution helped us to carry out this critical revitalization project and to launch a formal Exhibition Program.

The first exhibition and its catalogue would have been impossible without substantial support from many sources. Foremost among them is the J.M. Kaplan Fund, Inc. and its president, Joan Davidson, who generously provided for the publication of this book as well as for the series of public programs on censorship. Other grants that have assisted in the development of the exhibition have been provided by: the New York Times Company

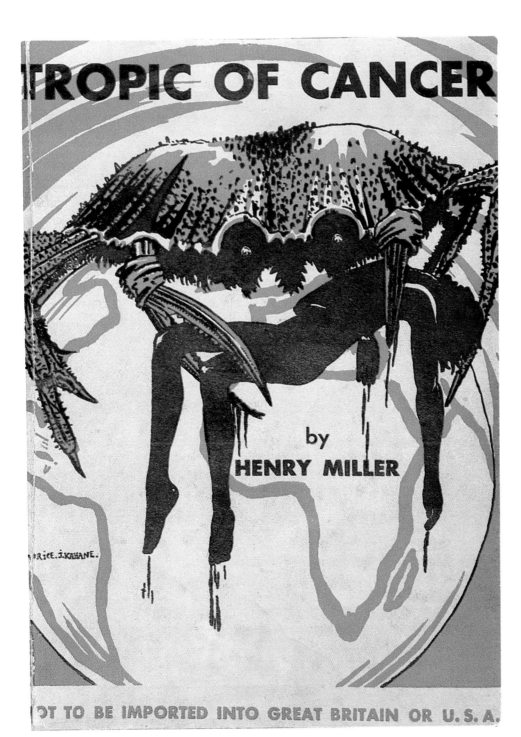

◀   Henry Miller, **Tropic of Cancer.** 1934.
Ex. no. 255

11

Foundation; the Exxon Corporation; the Philip L. Graham Fund; Time Inc.; and the New York State Council on the Arts.

Finally, I would like to express our appreciation for the encouragement and support the Library has received from the National Endowment for the Humanities during the initial development of the Exhibition Program and for the Endowment's grant that has made this exhibition possible.

During the restoration of the exhibition hall and throughout the development of the inaugural exhibition, the Library has received invaluable assistance from distinguished advisors. Sir John Pope-Hennessey, Consultative Chairman, Department of European Paintings, The Metropolitan Museum of Art, agreed to serve as Chairman and assembled an Advisory Committee to the Exhibition Program. The Committee, whose members are listed below, has been instrumental in advising the Library about planning the use of the Gottesman Exhibition Hall as a modern exhibition facility:

John Dobkin, National Academy of Design
Brendan Gill, New Yorker Magazine
Philip Johnson, Architect
Charles Ryskamp, The Morgan Library

A National Council of Advisors has also provided intellectual and artistic guidance during the development of the censorship program:

Robert Bernstein, Random House
Robert Darnton, Princeton University
Natalie Davis, Princeton University
Elizabeth Eisenstein, University of Michigan
Patricia Hills, Whitney Museum of American Art
Esther Katz, Institute for Research in History
Robert Lumiansky, New York University
Steven Marcus, Columbia University
Linda Nochlin, City University of New York
Joan Rosenbaum, Jewish Museum
Arthur Schlesinger, Jr., City University of New York
Richard Sennett, New York Institute for the Humanities
Warren Susman, Rutgers University
John Tedeschi, Newberry Library
Gordon Wright, Stanford University

To each we extend our thanks, and reiterate our hope that their association with the Library will continue to be a close one. We are particularly indebted to Arthur Schlesinger, Jr. for his affection and support for the Library, and for his preface to this book of essays.

Censorship: 500 Years of Conflict is the product of extensive curatorial collaboration among the aforementioned advisors, visiting scholars, and the Library's own specialists. Under the leadership of David Stam, Andrew W. Mellon Director of The Research Libraries, staff at all levels have worked alongside curatorial consultants to identify, prepare, and interpret the items chosen for the exhibition. The curatorial team was led by Ann Ilan Alter of The Institute for Research in History, whose expertise in European history was complemented by the work of American historian William Joyce, Assistant Director for the Rare Books and Manuscripts Division, The New York Public Library, and James Cuno, Assistant Professor of Art History, Vassar College. Others who contributed substantially to the curatorial work include Robert Rainwater, Keeper of Prints for the Library, and Richard Newman, Special Projects Researcher for the Exhibition Program.

We would like to acknowledge the special contributions of the following members of The New York Public Library staff: Gregory Long, Vice-President for Development and Public Relations; Terry Tegarden, Registrar;

Miriam de Arteni, Exhibition Conservator; Patricia Schwartz, Assistant, Exhibition Program; Christine Zvokel, Research Assistant; Francis O. Mattson, Susan Davis, Miriam Mandelbaum, John Rathe, and John Stinson of the Rare Books and Manuscripts Division; Donald Anderle, Associate Director, Special Collections; Jonathan Seliger, Print Collection; Bernard McTigue, Curator of the Arents Collections; David Cronin, Public Programs Coordinator; Lola Szladits, Curator of the Berg Collection; Genevieve Oswald, Curator of the Dance Collection; Jack LaFond, Intern in the Exhibition Program; Louis Mintz, Stan Kruger, and Larry Cuyler of Stack Maintenance and Delivery.

Scholar-specialists from other institutions who have helped with aspects of the project include: Norman Kleeblatt, Jewish Museum; William Preston, John Jay College; and Donald Reynolds. We would like to express special appreciation to The Institute for Research in History, whose scholars and staff have played an important role in the project. Of special note are the contributions of Katherine Crum and Marjorie Lightman; other scholars affiliated with the Institute include Frank Mecklenburg; Martha Driver, Pace University; Atina Grossman, Mount Holyoke College; and Clara Lovett, Library of Congress. Marvin Ciporen provided valuable assistance on the exhibition captions and overviews.

We would also like to thank the architectural consultants who were responsible for the restoration of Gottesman Hall: Arthur Rosenblatt, Special Assistant to the President for Real Estate and Architecture; Lew Davis of Davis Brody & Associates; and Giorgio Cavaglieri. The designers of the exhibition, Charles Froom and his associate Richard Franklin, deserve special mention for their enthusiasm for this project.

Just as *Censorship: 500 Years of Conflict* is the Library's first major exhibition in recent years, so is this publication the first of its kind for the Library. We acknowledge the dedicated efforts of the editor, William Zeisel, Director of Editors & Scholars; the designer, Brian Rushton; and the photographer, Robert Rubic. John Miller, Special Assistant to the Director of The Research Libraries, and Tobin Sparling, Print Specialist, prepared the exhibition list. Most importantly, we thank the distinguished scholars and writers who contributed to this book. Their rich and diverse essays add a new dimension to the study of censorship and provide an illuminating commentary on the exhibition itself.

Lastly, the Library and I owe our gratitude to Diantha Schull, Coordinator of Exhibitions, whose leadership and hard work have made our Exhibition Program and the opening of the D. Samuel and Jeane H. Gottesman Hall a reality.

Censorship: 500 Years of Conflict symbolizes the resilience of the spirit of free inquiry. Hence, this exhibition gives us an opportunity also to celebrate learning and to highlight the traditional role and importance of libraries as preservers and purveyors of information and knowledge.

For this opportunity to serve the nation and help preserve its heritage, we owe a debt of gratitude to thousands of past and present benefactors of the Library and to the dedicated staff who, over eight decades, have reaffirmed the role of the Library so clearly stated at the entrance to the Central Research Library:

ON THE DIFFUSION OF EDUCATION AMONG THE PEOPLE REST THE PRESERVATION AND PERPETUATION OF OUR FREE INSTITUTIONS.

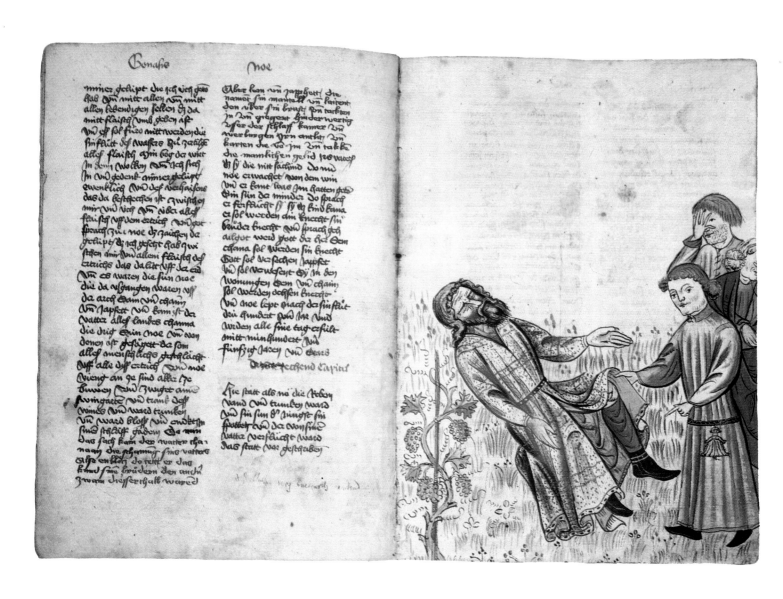

German manuscript Bible. 1445. Vernacular Bibles of this kind were becoming increasingly popular by the time of the Reformation. *Ex. no. 2*

1

In his novel *Julie, ou la Nouvelle Héloïse,* Jean-Jacques Rousseau touched on the sensitive and controversial subject of social and political equality. In a depth of emotion new to the eighteenth century, readers wept when Saint-Preux, the lover and tutor of the beautiful and aristocratic Julie, reproached her, "Deign to treat me more as an equal." The lesson of equality was a hard one. Yet, in a society still dominated by the aristocracy but where the bourgeoisie was beginning to assert its rights and privileges, the petition for equality struck home. In a second novel, published a year later, and condemned to the executioner's fire by the Parlement of Paris, Rousseau again touched on a theme that aroused passionate response among his readers. In *Emile* (1762) Rousseau described the birth, youth, and growing into adulthood of a child raised outside society. Untainted by greed or egoism, uncorrupted by civilization, and self-confident of his emotions, ability, and strength, Emile became a man ready to fulfill his role as a citizen of the dawning new age.

These two novels, among the most controversial and popular works of the eighteenth century, not only in France but in Europe generally, appear in the exhibition *Censorship: 500 Years of Conflict* because both were censored. Censorship did not, however, prevent these novels from reach-

An Introduction to the Exhibition

ANN ILAN ALTER

Tome II.   *Page 345.*

J. M. Moreau. Le jeune. invenit.   *1777*   *A. J. Duclos Sculpsit.*

ANN ILAN ALTER, a Fellow and founding member of The Institute for Research in History, is a cultural historian who has written on many aspects of European history, including history of fashion. In projects for various institutions, she has developed cross-cultural approaches to presenting history through the visual media.

◄   Jean-Jacques Rousseau, **Julie, ou La Nouvelle Héloïse.** 1774. A bestseller despite being censored in France, *Julie* went through at least fifty editions between 1761 and 1789. *Ex. no. 93*

IL PRENCIPE
DI NICOLO MA:
CHIAVELLI,

Al Magnifico Lorenzo di Piero
de Medici.

Con alcune altre operette, i titoli delle quali trouerai nella
seguente facciata.

IN PALERMO
Appresso gli heredi d'Antoniello dagli Antonielli
a xxviij. di Gennaio, 1584.

Machiavelli, **The Prince.** 1584.
Although the title page indicates it was
printed in Italy, this book was actually
produced in London and distributed
clandestinely throughout Europe. *Ex. no. 73*

Martin Marprelate, **Oh Read ouer D.
John Bridges, for It Is a Worthy Worke.** 1588.
Ex. no. 23

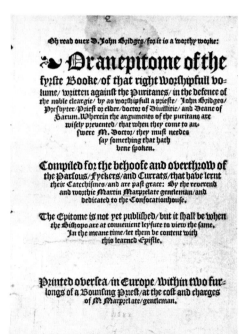

ing the reading public. Nor did it succeed in suppressing other books printed in France, or elsewhere in Europe, or in America. For century after century, controversial ideas have found their readers despite official banning, harassment, confiscation, and book burning. This remarkable endurance merits our careful scrutiny, for it has preserved from the censor's scissors many great works of the mind.

The exhibition *Censorship: 500 Years of Conflict* displays nearly 300 of the many printed works and images that have been censored in the West during the past five centuries. The exhibition demonstrates the power of ideas to survive. Its major themes are the intimate relationship between censorship and threats to the social, religious, or intellectual order; the changing face of censorship over time and cultures; and the ability of well-meaning individuals and institutions to persuade themselves that they are not really censoring.

At the heart of the exhibition lie the works themselves, the books, pamphlets, newspapers, broadsides, and prints. They are survivors, sometimes torn or mutilated, of the war of conflicting ideas and ideals. John Milton's *Areopagitica*, with its advocacy of a free press, is in the exhibition, as is a copy of Luther's German translation of the Bible, which helped spread ideas that altered the political and spiritual face of Europe and, ultimately, North America. Exhibited are copies of the Catholic *Index of Prohibited Books*, and some of the books that it tried to suppress. Also displayed are scores of polemical and satirical prints, including some that were censored, which used the press, a medium invented for the spread of words, to make the visual image into a means of mass communication and propaganda.

Although censorship was applied sporadically to printed works almost as soon as printing was invented, ca. 1455, no systematic method of controlling the flow of printed information came into being until after Luther posted his 95 Theses. When Pope Leo X condemned Luther's teachings, in the bull *Contra Errores*, Luther publicly burned a copy of the document. News of his act traveled across Europe, carried by merchants, journeymen, humanists, and soldiers, who passed pamphlets, vernacular Bibles, and Protestant and humanist tracts to friends and comrades-in-arms. As various reformers, thinkers, and writers began to pull at the threads of dogma and traditional tenets, censorship focused on the ever-growing number of Protestant vernacular versions of the Bible, many of which were condemned by the authorities: Estienne's in France, Luther's in Germany, and Tyndale's in England (all in the exhibition). Religious criticism led to political criticism, a threat few rulers could ignore. Machiavelli's *The Prince*, Anabaptist tracts, and Rabelais' *Gargantua* are examples of this threat.

Both Catholics and Protestants applied censorship to printed materials they found dangerous or subversive. As the exhibition makes clear, however, the effect was not so much to choke off this literature as to drive it underground, where it experienced a remarkable vitality and staying power. The Huguenot pamphlet *Vindiciae contra Tyrannos* (on exhibit) was published in Edinburgh (1579) for French readers; it provided a justification for revolt against unjust princes, in the name of Calvinist rectitude. This well-known clandestine pamphlet was republished a century later by Puritan rebels in England: it justified their revolt against and eventual regicide of Charles I (1649). Also in the exhibition are two pamphlets, the Martin Marprelate tracts, "printed overseas, in Europe, within two furlongs of a bouncing priest," that are Puritan satires on the role of bishops in enforcing censorship decrees in Elizabethan England. Although obvious targets of the laws they satirized, the tracts were widely available.

Starting in the late sixteenth century, printed works enjoyed, if anything, even greater immunity from effective control. An entire clandestine network of distribution had been organized, stretching from London to Cracow, Copenhagen to Rome. Authors frequently evaded censorship controls by having their works printed in another country or city. Descartes' *Discours sur la methode,* Locke's *On Toleration,* Milton's *Pro Populo Defensio,* and Cornelis Dusart's satires of Louis XIV and his prelates, *Les heros de la ligue,* were all published in the Netherlands. Printing had become an international business, immune to censors because of the heterogeneity of European life and the lack of political cohesion. Surviving well into the eighteenth century, these networks served several generations of writers and fed intellectual debates across Europe.

The period between 1650 and 1750 witnessed a consolidation and rationalization of state power in much of Europe. Even so, bureaucracies and police were ill-prepared to deal with the growing disenchantment that spread through Europe beginning in the 1760s. Thus, in eighteenth-century France, the breakdown of a political consensus among the elite destroyed the power base of the government and rendered censorship unenforceable.

By the time Rousseau published *Emile,* in 1762, the French monarchy was reluctant to let the opposition voice its opinions. The end of the Seven Years' War in 1763, and the financial crisis that ensued, quickly put events beyond the power of the king to control. A growing undercurrent of radical thought, during the 1770s and 1780s, produced many books and pamphlets that seemed more threatening to the established authorities than *Emile* or *Julie.* Many are in the exhibition. One is the Abbe Raynal's *Histoire philosophique et politique des établissements et du commerce dans les deux Indes,* a scathing radical critique of the European exploitation of the West Indies; it was immediately seized and condemned. Even more alarm-

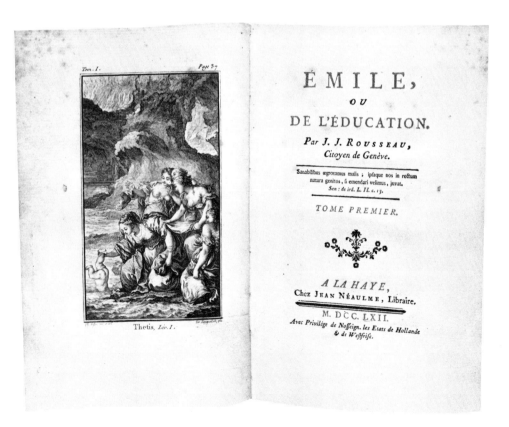

◀ Jean-Jacques Rousseau, **Emile, ou de l'Education.** 1762. Published clandestinely, it was condemned by the Parlement de Paris and burned. *Ex. no. 94*

17

ing was the torrent of Grub Street novels that used stories of sexual scandal to decry the immorality of the aristocracy and the monarchy. The *Memoirs authentiques de la Comtesse de Barreé* was a popular pornographic account of the life of the Comtesse du Barry, then Louis XV's mistress. Charles Thévenot de Morande, in the *Gazetier cuirassé,* offered gossip about the sexual exploits and proclivities of the aristocracy in and around the court. Guillaume Imbert's aptly titled *Chronique scandaleuse* was another salacious account of life among the privileged.

The police tried unsuccessfully to stop this traffic. Police spies notwithstanding, a censored book was a commercially successful book. Where the public was willing to pay, booksellers stepped in ready to sell. With title pages bearing "published 100 leagues from the Bastille under the sign of Liberty," or the like, these books satisfied the desires of an increasingly literate public, critical of the government yet with no legiti-

▼ Charles Thévenot de Morande, **Le Gazetier cuirassé.** 1771. Secretly published "100 leagues from the Bastille under the sign of Liberty," this was a salacious account of life among the nobility. *Ex. no. 125*

Aetna haec impavido vulcania tela ministrat
tela Gigantaeos Debellatura furores

Pembroke

L E

Gazetier Cuiraſſé:

Morande (Charles Thévenau de)

O U

Anecdotes Scandaleuſes

D E L A

COUR de FRANCE.

——— *Nous autres ſatiriques,*
Propres à relever les ſottiſes du tems;
Nous ſommes un peu nés pour être mécontens.
BOILEAU.

Imprimé à cent licües de la Baſtille à l'en-
ſeigne de la liberté.

MDCCLXXI.

mate outlet to vent their criticism. Authors claiming to write from "corners where one can see everything" allegedly revealed the truth about the monarchy and its corruption. Between these pages is to be found the most plausible explanation of why France was teetering. When it fell—along with censorship, which collapsed in 1788—the writers of this scurrilous literature moved from pornographic diatribes to political diatribes. The readers of their generation saw little difference.

The French Revolution did not restore an intellectual or social consensus to France. In England and the United States, however, a new consensus was emerging that was to have a deep impact on censorship. One of the exhibition's themes is how Victorian attitudes led to an internalized, unofficial, but effective censorship in England and the United States. Today we tend to think of it as a form of prudishness, but it was actually much more far-reaching. It resulted from social and economic developments—industrialization, urbanization, growing literacy and levels of education—that are associated with the rise of an expanding middle class. As this class imposed its values on society (excluding the poor, industrial workers, immigrants, and blacks), it turned private virtue into public virtue. By the 1830s a new ideology confidently proclaimed the preeminence of family, hard work, propriety, prudence, sexual restraint, and sentimentality. For the next six decades a moral urgency on both sides of the English-speaking world impelled editors, writers, heads of circulating libraries, and publishers to scrutinize every work for indelicate references or overly realistic portrayals of life. There may have been more censorship, self-imposed or otherwise, during that century, in England or in the United States, than during all the preceding centuries of printed literature.

The exhibition presents many examples of Victorian censorship. For example, new laws in both England and the United States prevented the distribution of birth-control literature that had previously been available. Charles Knowlton's *Fruits of Philosophy* (1825), one of the earliest books

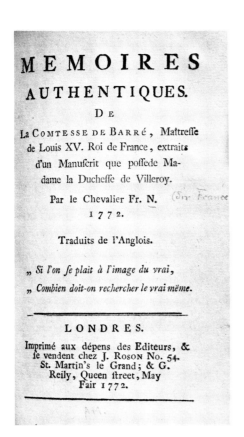

◀ Le Chevalier Fr. N., **Memoires authentiques de la Comtesse de Barrée.** 1772. These "authentic" memoirs were in reality a scathing attack on the French monarchy and court. *Ex. no. 126*

▶ Guillaume Imbert, **Chronique scandaleuse.** 1785. Like many works of its time, Imbert's book used licentious and scandalous tales to criticize the French monarchy and aristocracy. *Ex. no. 124*

on birth control, was now classified as obscene or indecent. Prosecutions of persons who distributed birth-control literature—Edward Bond Foote, *Borning Better Babies*, in the United States, and Annie Besant and Charles Bradlaugh, in England, for distributing Knowlton's book—successfully prevented such information from reaching women who wanted it. In the United States, despite the demand for them, birth-control devices and information were seized under the Comstock Laws—for example, Margaret Sanger's articles "What Every Girl Should Know."

While private virtue led to the imposition of public virtue in England and the United States, the French made a genuine effort, especially after 1815, to distinguish between the two. Rousseau's spiritual children—professionals, businessmen, rentiers, industrialists, intellectuals, scientists, moralists, and physicians, in short, the ideologues of bourgeois

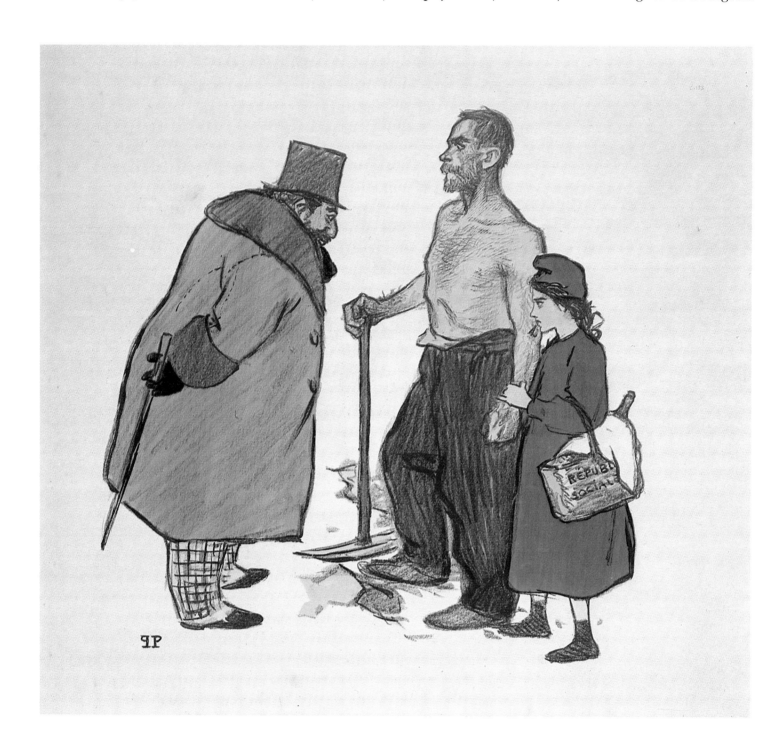

▼   Théophile Alexandre Steinlen, **La Cadette.** 1894. Stencil colored lithograph. In this print, socialist artist Steinlen attacked social and economic inequalities under capitalism. *New York Public Library: Art, Prints and Photographs.*

◀ **Sanger Clinic.** Ca. 1916. Photograph.
Ex. no. 217

◀ William Makepeace Thackeray, **Letter to
Elizabeth Barrett Browning.** April 2, 1861. As
editor of the family magazine *The Cornhill*,
Thackeray rejected for publication many
stories and poems he thought indecent or
indelicate. One of them was Browning's poem
Lord Walter's Wife. Ex. no. 176

36 Onslow Sqt. April 2. 1861.

My dear kind Mrs Browning

Has Browning ever had an aching Tooth wh. must come out (I dont say a Mrs Browning, for women are much more courageous) — a Tooth wh. must come out and wh. he has kept for months and months away from the dentist? I have had such a tooth a long time, and have sat down in the chair, and never had the courage to undergo the pull.

This tooth is an allegory (I mean this one) — Its your poem that you sent me months ago — and who am I to refuse the poems of Elizabeth Browning, and set myself up as a judge over her? I cant tell you how often I have been going to write, and have failed.

You see that our Magazine is written not only for men and women, but for boys, girls, infants, sucklings almost; and one of the best wives, mothers, women in the world writes some verses, wh. I feel certain would be objected to by many of our readers — Not that the writer is not pure

Gustave Flaubert, **Madame Bovary.**
1896. Flaubert was charged with immorality
and lasciviousness for publishing this novel
about the passions of a married woman in a
provincial town. When Flaubert was acquitted,
the book became an instant bestseller. Women
all over France wrote him to say he had
described their lives. *Ex. no. 178*

representative government—were aware of the role of virtue in building a new society. They tempered their republican virtue, however, with the aristocratic values they freely copied after 1789. Unlike England, family life in France was not idealized as the focus of social activity for both parents and children. Children were seen as little barbarians, to be shaped and molded into citizens, unfit for adult company. It should come as no surprise, then, that *Mademoiselle de Maupin*, Theodore Gautier's paean to sensuality, unavailable in England until 1887 and banned in the United States until Word War I, met criticism for immorality when it was published in Paris in 1835, but not censorship. In his preface, Gautier argued that novels satisfied a spiritual need and not a moral one. When the authorities tried to impose moral censorship, they failed. The trial of *Madame Bovary* (1856-57, first American edition, 1896) for lasciviousness and immorality made a bestseller of a novel that might otherwise have reached only a small audience. Acquitted, Gustave Flaubert became a hero to women all over France, who wrote him that he had described the morals of the provinces they lived in and the lives they led. The authorities reserved censorship primarily for the works of republicans, socialists, Saint-Simonians, and general attacks on the government such as the caricatures of Daumier and Philipon.

Meanwhile, the cultural and political consensus that made Victorian censorship so effective in England and the United States was beginning to break down. This happened first in England, where a new freedom became evident by the 1890s, when books which would have been prosecuted for obscenity a few years earlier, like Zola's novels, encountered no official opposition. In the United States, society was changing. Increased immigration, especially from southern and eastern Europe, turned whole neighborhoods of American cities and towns into foreign enclaves. Often barely able to speak English and unfamiliar with American social mores and manners, these immigrant men, women, and children filled the factories that fueled an industrializing nation. Women, many of them feminists, led social reform movements that brought to the immigrants and the poor the social services and education otherwise unavailable in crowded cities. During the same decades a radical critique of capitalism in America also began to be heard. In the face of radical activities led by the Socialist party, the Industrial Workers of the World *(One Big Union)*, and anarchist groups, the federal government expanded the formal constraints on expression and added new ones. Stephen Crane's *Maggie, A Girl of the Streets* was refused publication, and later appeared only with expurgations, which Crane felt took the teeth out of the novel. Dreiser's *Sister Carrie* was never distributed to bookstores, while his later novels, *The Titan* and *The Genius*, were withdrawn from bookstores under pressure.

Radicals were routinely arrested and radical literature confiscated and destroyed. With the entry of the United States into World War I, laws against radical political groups and publications, such as the I.W.W. and *The Masses*, made it treasonous to oppose United States participation in the war (*Sedition Law*, 1918), while patriotic citizens were exhorted to report any "seditious" activities in their neighborhoods. The general desire to control expression did not make fine distinctions between radicals and reformers or among immigrants of any kind: it prosecuted them all in an effort to preserve unity in fighting the war.

Following World War I, the United States and Western European governments responded to what they perceived as the threat of an international communist conspiracy. The Spartacist uprising in Germany, the occupation of the factories by socialists and communists in Northern

Italy, and the organization of the Third International were seen to confirm their fears. The name of national security was invoked to justify witch hunts, surveillance, and attacks on radicals and their works. Yet, despite this awesome attack on political free expression in the United States, by the 1920s changing values loosened the hold of Victorian censorship. In 1934, James Joyce's *Ulysses*, declared obscene in 1920 when segments were published in Margaret Anderson's *Little Review*, was legally cleared of the charge of obscenity. This was the first in a series of decisions, climaxing with *Lady Chatterley's Lover* in 1958, that opened the way for the virtual end of moral censorship in the United States.

In the meantime, a new threat to freedom of expression reared its head: fascism rendered freedom of expression and political choice obsolete. All citizens living under fascism were expected to give themselves to the state and its ideology. Members of the opposition suffered arrest, being jailed in Italy and placed in concentration camps in Germany, while the pervasiveness of the Nazi state required strict censorship and the confiscation of all clandestine literature. This policy failed, as examples in the exhibition of clandestine literature smuggled into Germany show. Despite book burnings of "decadent" authors and the threat of concentration camps, brave men and women distributed anti-Nazi news and information throughout Germany and occupied Europe. Not even the Nazi war machine had the technological means to crush clandestine networks.

The heroism of the war resistance was not the end of the story of censorship in the West, nor is it of the exhibition. By the late 1940s, the world was beginning to divide into geopolitical units disconcertingly similar to those described by George Orwell in his novel *1984*. As the decades have unfolded, Orwell's vision of the future has followed us persistently, reinforced by rapid strides in technological sophistication that he could have seen only dimly but whose significance he sensed. Orwell describes a society where printing has given way to television and electronic means as the primary mode of communication. Every day the state rewrites history and destroys the evidence of the past, a process so routine that censorship has become the norm. People—they are not really citizens any longer—have lost the ability and the desire to resist the state by appropriating the means of communication. Indeed, they have forgotten how.

It is important that we do not forget "how." It is important for us to remember our history: that the printed objects in this exhibition survived because men and women risked their lives to obtain them, read them, and protect them. *Censorship: 500 Years of Conflict* is about our ways of struggling with controversial and unsettling ideas. It holds lessons . . . and warnings.

ACKNOWLEDGMENTS

For their help in preparing this exhibition
I would like to thank my co-curators, William
Joyce, Assistant Director for the Rare Books
and Manuscripts Division, The New York
Public Library, and James Cuno, Assistant
Professor of Art History, Vassar College.

2

The Advent of Printing

PAUL F. GRENDLER

PAUL F. GRENDLER, Professor of History at the University of Toronto, is the author of numerous books and articles on printing, censorship, and the Italian Renaissance generally. His most recent book is *Culture and Censorship in Latin Renaissance Italy and France* (London: Variorum Reprints, 1981); he also wrote the chapter on printing and censorship for the forthcoming *Cambridge History of Renaissance Philosophy*. His current project is a book entitled *How Giovanni Learned to Read: Schools and Textbooks in the Italian Renaissance and Catholic Reformation*.

One day in or about 1450, Johann Gutenberg pulled the first printed page from the first printing press. He was too busy and too harried by his creditors to pause to record that memorable date. But with this simple act he brought to fulfillment a process begun nearly four thousand years before, when ancient Mesopotamians used carved cylinder seals as a quick way of "signing" clay tablets. It was a process that saw a major innovation in medieval China, where texts were carved on wooden boards and used to print on paper. Gutenberg's contribution was to break the board of text into its constituent elements—the letters—which could then be reused in new combinations. No longer was it necessary to carve an entirely new board for each page of text: one simply rearranged the units of type into the new text.

The implications of the new technique were quickly appreciated, and a revolution in communications ensued. At no time was the revolution so dramatic or disruptive as during the first hundred years after Gutenberg. Over the span of one century the handwritten manuscript gave way to the printed page. The laborious duplication of information by hand yielded to a nascent technology of reproduction. An industry grew up not only to print books, pamphlets, drawings, and broadsides, but to distribute and sell them all over the Western world and to an ever-widening spectrum of the population. And as the deep changes wrought by printing began to appear, there also appeared the first serious attempts to enforce censorship of written works on a wide scale.

Gutenberg's first printed book of any size was the beautiful forty-two-line Bible, printed about 1455. But this famous Bible had mostly symbolic importance, for printing could not make a significant impact on the spread of ideas until presses were established in sufficient number and in major population centers and a broad system of distribution and marketing was in place. That point was reached between 1470 and 1480. Some nineteen European towns had printing presses by 1470; by 1500 some 255 towns had printers. Major printers had numerous presses. The number of books printed rose exponentially.

Johann Gutenberg and his associates at Mainz experimented for years before they were able to combine the technical processes necessary for printing. In perfecting their art they benefited from two earlier innovations. Between the first and fifth centuries A.D., the codex (a bound volume of flat, uniform-sized leaves) replaced the roll as the usual physical format of the book. Then paper came, from China through the Near East into the West, about 1100. It spread throughout Europe until, by the early fifteenth century, most manuscript books were written on paper. Paper suited printing far better than vellum (prepared animal skin): it was more pliable, absorbed ink better than vellum, and was considerably cheaper. The production of vellum could never have expanded sufficiently to satisfy the demand unleashed by the invention of printing, even if Europeans had been willing to sacrifice most of their livestock to the new art.

The printer had the great advantage over the scribe of the ability to produce numerous copies in a short period of time. The number of copies in a press run (i.e., a single edition or printing) was modest at first: the estimates of the press run for the Gutenberg Bible range from 70 to 270. The size of the press runs then grew. Press runs of about 1,000 were common perhaps as early as the 1480s, became the norm by 1500, and stayed at this figure for the sixteenth century. But individual press runs in the sixteenth century varied a great deal, from as few as 100 copies for commissioned works intended for limited distribution, to as many as 5,000 copies for books of great interest and anticipated high sales. Large

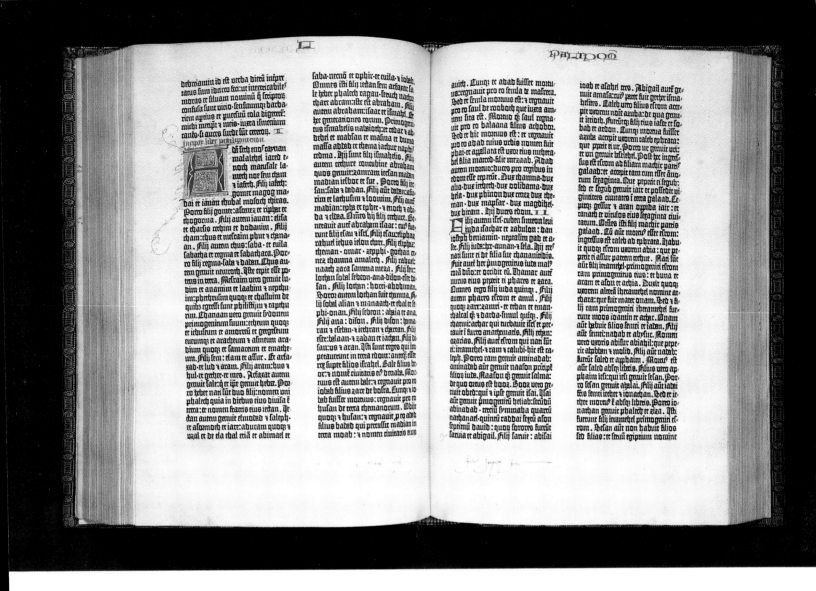

press runs helped Martin Luther spread his message: his *Address to the Christian Nobilty of the German Nation* (Wittenberg, 1520) had an initial press run of 4,000 copies plus numerous reprints.

Publishers usually did not risk a large first edition because of the high cost of printing and the lack of copyright protection, but when a title sold well, they quickly issued reprints. A popular title might go through numerous editions within a few years, both those issued by the original publisher and those of other publishers. The press runs or reprints were about the same size as first editions.

Book distribution became remarkably international. Regular and extensive commercial networks developed so that, for example, Venetian publishers shipped their books for sale in other Italian towns, Spain, England, France, Germany, Poland, and the Near East. Regional and international tradefairs played a key role in the international distribution of books. Frankfurt hosted the best-known fair, which met semi-annually for two or three weeks in the second half of Lent and in late summer, and attracted publishers, booksellers, and scholars from all over Europe.

Book prices were high at first (although never so high as the price of manuscripts) but soon dropped as the rate of production rose. Aldus Manutius published the first Greek edition of Aristotle's *Opera* in five volumes between 1495 and 1498, offering them for sale for 1½ to 3 ducats per volume and 11 ducats for the complete set. Since a humanist schoolmaster or university professor, in the faculty of arts, of modest reputation earned 50 to 100 ducats annually, he could afford the Greek Aristotle, although the outlay took a significant fraction of his annual income. But simple vernacular books such as a comedy, a volume of poetry, a devotional treatise, a work of history, or one of the ubiquitous vernacular translations of classical texts, sold for as little as 8 to 20 *soldi*. (There were 124 *soldi* to one ducat.) Such books were well within the means of artisans. In the second half of the sixteenth century, for example, a Venetian master mason earned 30 to 50 *soldi* per day; his assistant, 20 to 37 *soldi* daily. Hence, the artisan could afford to buy a few books—assuming he had the inclination and money after paying for food, housing, etc.

One reason for the gradual drop in book prices may have been the lack of an effective copyright system, which meant that publishers could "pirate" already published works without paying any copyright fees. An author, or more often the publisher, might obtain a copyright (called a "privilege") giving him exclusive publication rights for a short period of time (typically ten years). But the privilege was valid only within the political jurisdiction (city, princedom, etc.). A printer in another political jurisdiction, which might be a city only fifty miles away, could obtain a copy of the book and reprint it under his own name. For example, from 1509 through 1520, Erasmus' *Praise of Folly* appeared in at least thirty-five editions in nine different cities, printed by fourteen or more publishers. Only large and complicated books, such as those with technical illustrations, escaped pirating, because of the expense involved.

Authors and printers complained about the lack of copyright protection, but hastened to take advantage of the situation. A famous author like Erasmus could even profit from the publishers' piracy. After the first edition of a work of his appeared, rival publishers offered Erasmus money for a revised version. Erasmus obligingly made a few changes, wrote a new prefatory letter, and the publisher issued the work as a "new edition revised by the author." Readers then bought the new edition, leaving the

4.

IMPRESSIO LIBRORVM.

Poteſt vt vna vox capi aure plurima: Linunt ita vna ſcripta mille paginas.

original publisher and booksellers with unsold copies on their hands. A Paris publisher who had been victimized by Erasmus in this way complained to him—in vain—in 1516:

> Such is your reputation among your fellow-men, that if you announce a revised editon of any of your works, even if you have added nothing new, they will think the old edition worthless. Losses of this kind have been forced on me in respect of the *Copia*, the *Panegyricus*, the *Enchiridion* (I had undertaken for 500 copies), and the *Adagia*, of which I had bought 110. It would thus be greatly to our advantage if you would assign each individual work to a single printer, and not revise it until he had sold off all the copies.

Actually, neither Erasmus' nor Luther's views could have spread so quickly had pirating publishers been obliged to obtain permission to reprint, and to pay for the right. Books of less inflammatory subject matter also enjoyed the same wide diffusion. A good edition of Cicero's *Epistulae ad familiares (Letters to His Friends)*, a text used in schools across Europe, could be reprinted at will. It meant that teachers and students everywhere could use the text at small cost, because unrestricted reprinting probably drove down the price.

Lower prices meant more people could afford to own books. In the age before printing, few individual libraries were large: the great humanist Petrarch had about 200 titles when he died in 1374—a magnificent collection by fourteenth-century standards. But the average library was very small. A fifteenth-century scholar or professional, such as a physician, owned only a handful of books, and the merchant, shopkeeper, or elementary school teacher would be lucky to own a book of hours, a devotional work, and perhaps a book of tables for money exchange.

Printing changed this dramatically. Fernando Columbus of Seville (d. 1539), the natural son of the explorer, had 15,000 titles. A university

◀ Theodore Galle, **Printing Office.** Ca. 1600. Engraving. *Ex. no. 86*

▶ Erasmus, **In Praise of Folly.** 1520. A humanist who favored reform within the church, Erasmus was classified by the Inquisition as an author "of the second class," which meant that his work could be read only if "objectionable" parts were expurgated. *Ex. no. 31*

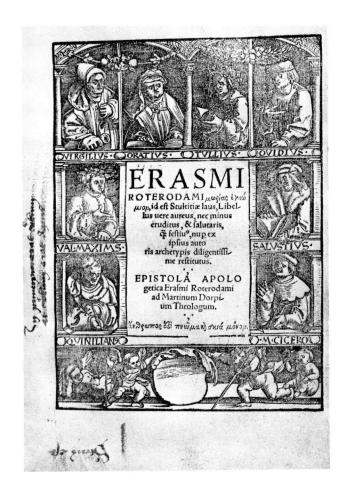

27

humanities professor or lawyer of average income for his profession could own a good working collection of up to 100. Many more shopkeepers and merchants now owned vernacular books, as many as a dozen: chivalric romances, devotional treatises, saints' lives, a chronicle or history, a commercial arithmetic, and the Bible in some form.

The astonishing multiplicity of books produced by the printing press greatly facilitated the mastery of basic skills that were the prerequisites for learning. Early printers probably printed far more Latin grammars than any other kind of book, allowing schoolchildren and adult learners to own printed copies of elementary reading texts and Latin grammars. The same was true for other kinds of textbooks: the classics, the books read in university, arithmetics, technical manuals, vernacular self-help books, and even letter-writing manuals. Relatively few copies of these humble products of the printer's art survive, but they were enormously important to the age—and profitable for the printers.

Printing also contributed to the speed and extent of scholarly and scientific discourse. The printed book allowed the unlimited duplication of text and illustrations. A manuscript was unique; it required an artist of equal skill to copy it, and his copy would not necessarily be identical. Printing allowed the exact reproduction of thousands of identical illustrations. The medical student could learn something of anatomy without dissecting corpses. Geometrical drawings in mathematical works, pictures of plants in books of botany, illustrations of animals in works of zoology, maps in geographies, and diagrams of mechanical contrivances in books of technology contributed greatly to these fields.

Printing freed all readers—scholars, clerics, merchants, mechanics, and all the rest—from geographical constraints. The London reader could easily own books printed in Basel. Indeed, a sign of the geographical freedom conferred by the press is that few university towns became major publishing centers, while many commercial and population hubs did.

But printing also intensified controversy in an already contentious age. Before printing, debates—a major form of intellectual exchange—were relatively personal and limited: two men engaged in a public disputation in an academic setting, or they exchanged letters. Only a small audience heard or read their words initially, and it took time for their words to spread. Not so after printing, which offered the opportunity to respond again and again to an ever-widening audience. Now everyone with a facility in Latin or a vernacular language could follow the major political and religious discussions of the day. Now anyone having access to a press could join the debate as quickly as the author could write and the printer print. Sometimes this was a matter only of days.

The Renaissance and Reformation produced many brilliant minds, for example Erasmus and Machiavelli, but perhaps the one who first really grasped the possibilities of the press to change the world was Martin Luther. Luther seemed made for the press. He wrote as he spoke: effortlessly in a style that combined passion, sincerity, great energy, homely examples, and original insight. Luther wrote from the heart in highly emotional terms as he explained, out of the depths of his own struggle for salvation, the pathway for others. He had the gift of cutting through centuries of tradition to focus on the great issue of humankind's lonely relationship with God.

Luther's books defy structural analysis because he seemed to speak spontaneously from the heart, and because he expanded his original principles in open debate. Opponents who attempted to answer him according to late-medieval principles of argument found it a frustrating experience. Luther did not allow for qualification; he said everything with absolute certainty that included a relentless, frontal assault on those who differed with him. Luther never conceded any goodwill on the part of his opponents, a quality that made him more effective as a polemicist. Above all, there was his inexhaustible energy. An opponent would no sooner finish answering one book than discover that Luther had written three more in the interim. It is impossible to imagine the Protestant Reformation without Luther, and equally impossible to imagine it succeeding without the printing press to spread his words.

The power of Luther's words brought forth an immediate response from his temporal and civil ruler, the emperor Charles V, whose Edict of Worms (May 26, 1521) contained a "Law of Printing," which prohibited the printing, sale, possession, reading, or copying of Luther's works. Luther himself endorsed censorship and acknowledged the power of the written word when he urged his immediate temporal lord, the Elector of Saxony, to prohibit the writings of Andreas Bodenstein von Karlstadt, a follower who had gone further and faster than Luther in breaking from Catholicism. These initial attempts to censor controversial works had little effect, however, for various reasons. For one thing, many intellectuals still held to the optimistic Renaissance view of human potentiality. One might read "bad" books, such as ancient classical literature that praised paganism and portrayed vice attractively, and pick out what was "good." Another factor limiting the effectiveness of censorship was the multiplicity of states in Europe at that time, making it difficult to enforce a law or decree over more than a very limited region. Finally, there was the general bureaucratic inefficiency and fragmentation of authority, which hampered the ability of large institutions to enforce their will.

This is not to say that writers could proceed as if there was no censorship at all, for they were liable to heavy penalties for producing works that might offend powerful interests. Governments had an unspoken political censorship: a subject did not openly criticize his rulers and their policies, and could suffer punishment—even death—if he did so. In 1428, for example, a friend urged Guarino Guarini of Verona, a famous humanist, to write the history of a recently concluded war between Venice and Milan. Guarino, a Venetian subject, declined. He referred approvingly to Cicero's famous dictum that history is the "light of truth" (*De oratore*, ii. 9. 36) but went on to add that following the light could be dangerous. As soon as the historian laid bare the causes of the war, Guarino observed, and the virtues (and vices) of the contestants, he would pay for the truth with his head.

Although Guarino might fear the wrath of his rulers, he no doubt shared the prevailing view among humanists that in the final analysis the individual had to decide what was good and what was not. This rather benevolent view began to change under the pressure of events during the Reformation, as the printed word was used increasingly as a weapon in a great struggle. Catholic and Protestant authorities, locked in a bitter struggle with each other, concluded that only some form of systematic press censorship could curb the spread of "unacceptable" religious and political views. A foretaste of the new intolerance occurred in 1553, when across Italy copies of the Talmud and other Hebrew books were burned for their alleged anti-Christian sentiments, and surviving copies were often censored. (Printing in Hebrew survived, but the Talmud was not published again in Renaissance Italy.)

Under the conditions prevailing in sixteenth-century Europe, effective press censorship had to include three components. First, a catalogue

Contra hebreos retinentes libros in quibus aliquid contra fidem catholicam notetur vel scribatur.

Romæ apud Antonium Bladum Impressorem Cameralem.

▲ **Papal decree** forbidding the possession of books written in Hebrew. 1554. *Ex. no. 24*

▼ Solomon ben Abraham Adret, **Teshuvot she'elot leha-RaSH BA.** Before 1480. This collection of *responsa*—decisions in Jewish law—bears the signatures of three church censors who read it: Girolamo da Durallano, Luigi da Bologna, and Giovanni Dominico Carretto. *Ex. no. 33*

identifying offensive books, authors, and ideas was needed. Second, prepublication censorship had to halt the printing of offensive works within an individual state (principality, republic, duchy, etc.), a task in which church and state usually collaborated by appointing readers to examine manuscripts, and grant (or deny) permission to print. Third, to control the commerce in books, all imported printed materials had to be inspected (usually at the customs house), and bookstores had to be visited periodically to ensure that the owners were following the law against distributing proscribed works.

Both Catholic and Protestant authorities used these same techniques of censorship. Churchmen took the lead in pointing out heretical books, while civil authorities enforced the prohibitions through the police powers of the state. Both civil and religious leaders viewed heresy as an intolerable evil endangering humankind's salvation and threatening to incite civil rebellion. Heresy seemed to threaten the kingdoms of both heaven and earth.

After several abortive attempts, the papacy in 1564 promulgated an *Index librorum prohibitorum (Index of Prohibited Books)*, usually called the *Tridentine Index* because it had been authorized by the Council of Trent. With this *Index* the supreme spiritual authority of Catholicism defined which books and authors could not be printed or read by Catholics. It consisted of several parts: a long list of authors whose entire output was prohibited; an additional list of banned individual titles; rules for expurgation of books containing some error but whose "chief matter" was "good"; and sweeping rules for the regulation of the book trade. The major reason for prohibition was doctrinal error, that is, a book propagated Protestant ideas. But the *Tridentine Index* also banned some anti-clerical, lascivious, pornograhic, and political works, such as those of Machiavelli, as well as books of magic, demonology, and other occult arts. Individual papal decrees banning new titles, plus revision of the *Index* approximately once every fifty years, kept it up to date.

▶ **Index of Prohibited Books.** 1559. With the beginning of the Counter-Reformation the Inquisition persecuted heretics with increased intensity. One of the means to stamp out heresy was to suppress heretical books and tracts. This *Index* was the first list of prohibited books published by the Roman Catholic Church. Shown here are the title page and a page on which Martin Luther is listed as a prohibited author. *Ex. no. 28*

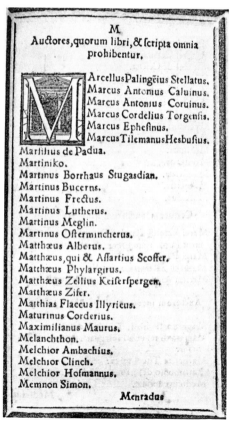

Protestant censorship also became sterner after mid-century, following the same pattern as Catholic censorship with minor differences in emphasis and organization. Because most Protestant religious leaders invested the state with substantial authority over the church, the state assumed the leading role in censorship. England is a prime example; the crown defined heresy, issued censorship regulations, and relied on civil agencies to enforce them.

◄ Portrait of Henry VIII from **Great Bible of Henry VIII.** 1539. Based on a translation into English by William Tyndale, this Bible was to be the official version used in the newly reformed Church of England. Since printing techniques in England were less advanced than those abroad, it was decided to print the book in Paris. French authorities protested and tried to stop the Bible from being printed. Sheets of the book, smuggled out of France in hats, were taken to England where the printing was completed. The Great Bible was distributed to every church in England, with the king's instructions that each man should interpret scripture for himself. *Ex. no. 17*

◄ **Proclamation of King Henry VIII** establishing that every English church should have a copy of the Great Bible. 1541. *Ex. no. 18*

The religious divisions within Protestant ranks meant that other Protestant titles as well as Catholic works were often prohibited. A Lutheran state might not permit the publication of Calvinist books within its borders and vice-versa; both Lutheran and Calvinist states normally prohibited the books of Anabaptists (the left-wing of the Reformation consisting of Mennonites, Hutterites, and other sectarian groups). Finally, because of the fragmentation of Protestant Europe, its censorship failed to achieve the comprehensiveness of Catholic censorship: Protestant states did not issue indexes and could not censor beyond local political boundaries. Perhaps for this reason Protestants censored the press less effectively than did Catholics. This is only a surmise, because Protestant censorship has been little studied.

As a result of censorship, the press, with a handful of exceptions, split along religious lines. Nevertheless, those who wanted prohibited books got them. Book smuggling was so widespread that it might more accurately be termed "the clandestine trade" that supplemented the open commerce. Members of the book trade bought prohibited books in Frankfurt and then shipped them along with innocent volumes through normal channels. The carrier, the man who accompanied shipments of books over long distances, was a key figure. He hid away a few contraband volumes amidst hundreds of legitimate books. Then he found ways to circumvent the inspection of his merchandise when he reached his destination: an easy-going inspector, a bribed official, or a false title page helped the books to slip through.

Censorship did not halt the communication of ideas, but it did severely hamper it. The sixteenth century lacked a concept of freedom of expression; it was too much to expect that from an age torn by religious and political strife. It would have to wait until the bitter upheaval of the Protestant Reformation was over.

▲ Cochlaeus, i.e., Johannes Dobnek of Wendelstein, **XXI Articuli Anabaptistarum Monasteriensium.** 1534. This book discusses the beliefs of the Anabaptists, a Reformation sect whose writings were censored by both Catholics and Protestants. *Ex. no. 21*

▼ Rabelais, **Gargantua.** 1547. Since Rabelais was classified by the Inquisition as an author "of the first class," his work was totally banned. *Ex. no. 29*

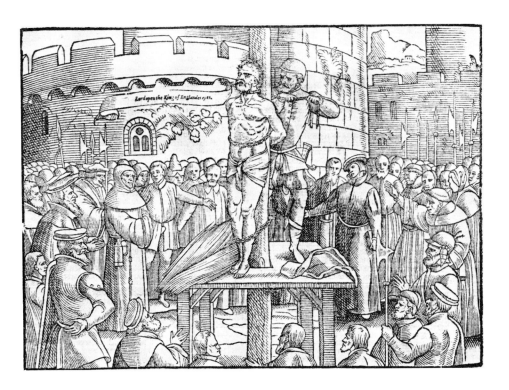

▲ John Foxe, **The Ecclesiasticall History,**
better known as **Foxe's Book of Martyrs.** Vol.
2. 1576. In his famous book, Foxe recounts the
lives of Protestants who suffered death for
their religious beliefs. The scene illustrated is
of the burning of William Tyndale, whose
translation of the Bible was condemned by the
Catholic church. *Ex. no. 14*

SOURCES

There is space to mention only a handful of
the very large number of good studies on the
printing press in its first century. Two
excellent surveys are the starting point:
Lucien Febvre, Henri-Jean Martin et al., *The
Coming of the Book. The Impact of Printing
1450-1800,* trans. David Gerard (London: NLB,
1976); and Rudolf Hirsch, *Printing, Selling and
Reading 1450-1550,* 2nd ed. (Wiesbaden: Otto
Harrassowitz, 1974). They brilliantly
synthesize the results of numerous detailed
studies. Curt F. Bühler describes with
sensitivity the transition from script to print:
*The Fifteenth Century Book. The Scribes, The
Printers, The Decorators* (Philadelphia:
University of Pennsylvania Press, 1960).
Martin Lowry sheds fresh light on how Aldus
Manutius managed to publish numerous first
editions of the classics and, at the same time,
to keep his head above water financially: *The
World of Aldus Manutius: Business and
Scholarship in Renaissance Venice* (Oxford:
Basil Blackwell, 1979). Leon Voet provides the
best information available about such practical
matters as prices, press runs, etc: *The Golden
Compasses: A History and Evaluation of the
Printing and Publishing Activities of the
Officina Plantiniana at Antwerp,* 2 vols.
(Amsterdam, London, and New York: 1969 and
1972). For the Frankfurt bookfair (which is still
in existence), see James Westfall Thompson,
*The Frankfurt Book Fair: The Francofordiense

emporium of Henri Estienne* (Chicago, 1911;
rpt. New York: Burt Franklin, 1968).

Although the history of press censorship
has not been studied so thoroughly, the
following are the key works. Almost all
sixteenth-century *Indices* have been reprinted
in Franz Heinrich Reusch, ed., *Die Indices
Librorum Prohibitorum des Sechzehnten
Jahrhunderts* (Tübingen, 1886; rpt.
Nieuwkoop: De Graaf, 1961). Reusch's
monumental other work provides a wealth of
information on banned books and authors: *Der
Index der Verbotenen Bücher: Ein Beitrag zur
Kirchen- und Literaturgeschichte,* 2 vols. in 3
parts (Bonn, 1883-84; rpt. Darmstadt, 1967).
Friedrich Kapp provides additional information
on German printing and censorship:
Geschichte des deutschen Buchhandels,
Vol. I (Leipzig: Börsenvereins der Deutscher
Buchhändler, 1886). Joseph Hilgers fills out
what Reusch missed: *Der Index der Verboten
Bücher* (Freiburg, 1904). For a study of how
censorship worked in practice in the most
important Italian publishing center, see Paul F.
Grendler, *The Roman Inquisition and the
Venetian Press 1540-1605* (Princeton:
Princeton University Press, 1977).

For the quotation containing the complaint
about Erasmus, see: Letter of Josse Bade,
September 29, 1516, in *The Correspondence
of Erasmus,* Vol. 4 (Toronto: University of
Toronto Press, 1977), Ep. 472.

Hiobs reichthum

ES war ein man im lande Vz/v
hies Hiob/der selb war schlecht vnd recht/G
fürchtig/vnd meidet das böse/vnd zenget sie
söne vnd drey töchter/Vnd seins viehes war
ben tausent schaf/drey tausent kamel/funff h
dert joch rinder/vnd funff hundert eselin/vnd
viel gesinds/Vnd er war mechtiger/denn alle
gegen morgen woneten.

Vnd seine söne giengen hin vnd machten mal/ein jglicher jnn
nem hause auff seinen tag/vnd sandten hin vnd luden jre drey sch
stern mit jnen zu essen vnd zu trincken. Vnd wenn ein tag des wc
bens vmb war/sandte Hiob hin vnd heiligete sie/vnd machte sich
morgens frue auff vnd opfferte Brandopffer/nach jr aller zal/D
Hiob gedachte/meine söne möchten gesundiget/vnd Gott gesege
haben jnn jrem hertzen. Also thet Hiob alle tage.

Es begab sich aber auff einen tag/da die kinder Gottes kan
vnd fur den HERRN tratten/kam der Satan auch vnter jnen. J
HERR aber sprach zu dem Satan/Wo komstu her? Satan antu
tet dem HERRN/vnd sprach/Ich hab das land vmbher durch
gen. Der HERR sprach zu Satan/Hastu nicht acht geh
auff meinen Knecht Hiob? Denn es ist sein gleiche nicht im l
de/schlecht vnd recht/Gottfürchtig/vnd meidet das böse. Sa
antwortet dem HERRN/vnd sprach/Meinstu/das Hiob v
sonst Gott fürchtet? Hastu doch jn/sein Haus vnd alles was er b
rin

*Hiobs lob so wie got
selbst zialt./*

3

Polemical Prints during the Reformation

CHRISTIANE ANDERSSON

Historians have rightly emphasized the enormous significance of the printing press—the principal means of disseminating Luther's theology—for the development of the Reformation as a mass movement. But the didactic and informative function of the press was not limited to texts, since the low rate of literacy in Germany at the beginning of the sixteenth century probably made the printing of images equally important. Luther himself recognized the potential persuasiveness of printed images, as demonstrated by the many tracts he had Wittenberg printers publish with illustrations produced in the workshop of his friend Lucas Cranach. Especially with regard to polemical statements, an image could convey an idea more succinctly and more incisively than words. The importance of printed pictures as polemical tools was generally recognized during the sixteenth century: images and texts carried equal responsibility and must have been considered equally dangerous or offensive. Censorship regulations consistently banned text and image together. Emperor Charles V, for example, in the Edict of Worms (1521), specified the materials subject to censorship as "both printed and illustrated," and included the artist along with the printer and author among those who would be punished for violating the edict's provisions. The Nuremberg town council, when banning offensive tracts, was especially careful to confiscate the woodblocks with which the illustrations had been printed.

Censorship of printed pictures was handled no differently from that of texts, because in Reformation propaganda they were often inseparable. Text and image were usually printed together on a single sheet of paper, a broadsheet (fig. 12), or, if the text extended to more than one page, bound together as a pamphlet (fig. 9); contemporary censorship regulations cite both types. Although painted banners, murals, and even wooden and bronze sculpture are occasionally mentioned as having been censored, items of printed propaganda greatly outnumbered those of any other medium, owing to the ability of the press to produce innumerable accurately replicated, easily transported, and inexpensive copies.

◀ **Martin Luther's translation of the Old Testament.** 1534. *Ex. no. 9*

▶ Luther, **Gnade unde Frede in Christo.** 1523. Printed broadsides helped spread Luther's message. This one urges the citizens of Stettin to live in accord with the Reformer's view of Christian virtue. *Ex. no. 36*

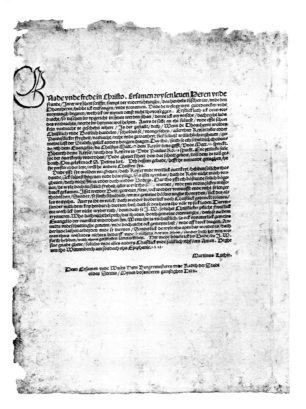

CHRISTIANE ANDERSSON, Assistant Professor in the Department of Art History and Archaeology at Columbia University, is currently on leave as a Guest Scholar at the J. Paul Getty Museum in Malibu, California. She has written widely on the influence of the Lutheran Reformation on German art, including an article on the work of Lucas Cranach the Elder in *Humanismus und Reformation als kulturelle Kräfte in der deutschen Geschichte*, ed. Lewis W. Spitz (Berlin: Historische Kommission, 1980). Two further studies are in press: "Popular Imagery in German Reformation Broadsheets" and "Polemical Prints in Reformation Nuremberg." Professor Andersson co-authored a recent catalogue for the exhibition, *From a Mighty Fortress: Prints, Drawings and Books in the Age of Luther*, shown at the Detroit Institute of Art, the National Gallery of Canada, and the Kunstsammlungen der Veste Coburg, West Germany in 1981-82. She is also the author of *Dirnen, Krieger, Narren: Ausgewählte Zeichnungen von Urs Graf* (Basel: Gute Schriften Verlag, 1978).

These objects of mass communication came under a variety of censorship laws. Imperial decrees set standards for all of Germany (at that time not a national state but an agglomeration of small states and free imperial cities, constituting a portion of the far-flung Holy Roman Empire). The crucial document is the Edict of Worms, promulgated in 1521 after Luther's appearance before the authorities for questioning about his controversial views on the church. The edict decreed the censorship of Luther's writings and of all printed material deemed contrary to the Catholic religion or directed against the pope, the prelates of the church, princes, or university faculties. Nothing injurious to these parties could be produced, bought, sold, or even owned, openly or secretly, and any libellous material already in existence was to be confiscated and publicly burned.

To enforce the edict, the emperor appointed professors of theology as his censors, but ultimately he depended on the various municipal councils, which had the right to issue their own regulations about censorship. These local ordinances tended to follow the wording of the Edict of Worms very closely, and usually established the town councillors as the local censoring body. The ordinances required printers to swear an oath of compliance with the rules, and to offer for inspection copies of everything intended for publication, so that permission to print could be given or refused. The punishments listed for contravening the regulations may appear unduly harsh, including, for example, heavy fines or exclusion from the printing profession, but one suspects that to some extent these guidelines were intended to dispel imperial suspicions about the willingness of towns to prosecute offenders. The actual decisions of the local magistrates often showed great leniency.

The division of authority to censor, between the emperor and the local magistrates, and the important role of the town councils in implementing imperial censorship decrees, could produce very complex situations when passionately held beliefs were at stake. The emperor was legally entitled

Quinta etas mundi

Res soles post morte Jul
exorti sunt z apparuerut i
n vnū corp⁹ solare redacti
couenerut:significates dominiū L
tonij atqz Augusti in vnā monarch
tius qz noticia trini z vni⁹ dei toti
Bos quoqz aranti in suburbano r
frustra se vzgeri quia in bzeui mag
esse qz frumenta.

Jbliotheca toto vrbe terrari
liū libzoz in egypto cõburif
tia in colligēdis libzis p veteres l
z bibliotheca z scolā Theophzast
fuit(vt Strabo arbitraf)qui libzo
pti reges bibliothece ordine docu
stus neleo tradidit. Neleus sceptin
peritos:qui libzos inclusos ac neg
nebant. Ptbolome⁹ quoqz pbilad
rū libzoz collegit. Et vt Seneca t
rū alexandrie arserunt pulcberrimi
nimentū:sicut z Liui⁹ qui elegant
giū id opus ait fuisse. Non fuit ele
sed studiosa luxuria:imo nec studi
diū sed in spectaculū cõparaueran
etiam seruiliū litterarū libzi non st
sed cenationū instrumenta sunt.

Salustius

Salustius romanus bistoricus ac pbilosopb⁹ Cicero
ruit. Js fuit nobilitate veritatis insignis bistoricus
catilinario:necnõ z de bello iugurtbino libzos edidit cele
psit epistolas.

Varro vico atice z narbonensi prouincia natus ro
fuit eruditissimus quidē z acutissimi ingenū vir:atq

to intervene only when printers of offensive material had successfully circumvented the local censors, at which point the damage was already done. Protestant towns, such as Nuremberg after 1524, had to maintain a delicate balance between tacit support of local Lutheran views and public gestures of support for the Catholic emperor. The degree to which local authorities enforced censorship regulations was always determined by the political cirumstances of the moment. A papal legate visiting Nuremberg in 1525 noted with surprised displeasure that the local magistrates willingly allowed the printing and dissemination of Lutheran tracts. But in 1549, after the Protestant forces had suffered defeat in the First Schmalkaldic War, the Nuremberg councillors denied permission to the printer Hans Guldenmund—known for his publishing of polemical materials—to issue a pamphlet on the Resurrection. They were, they explained laconically, "not inclined to allow very much to be printed at this time."

In 1530, convinced that his decrees on censorship were not achieving the desired effect, the emperor issued the Edict of the Diet of Augsburg, which introduced the requirement that all printed material identify its printer and place of publication. This would allow the imperial authorities to see at a glance which town councils had allowed offensive items to pass uncensored. A predictable result of this identification requirement was the invention or falsification of names: one broadsheet was supposedly printed in "Bethlehem near the Nile," and another one carried the name of a printer who must have been astonished and chagrined to discover his name in the colophon of a text he had never seen before. Sometimes the printer could be identified by a careful examination of the typeface, a method used, for example, during municipal proceedings in Basel against a tract written by the Strasbourg preacher Wolfgang Capito. A Basel printer testified under oath that the typeface in question could be traced to the Strasbourg printer Köpfl, who suffered imprisonment in the tower.

Hans Sebald Beham, **Biblische Historien figürlich fürbildet.** 1536. To reach the widest possible audience, books such as this Bible used images to augment text. *Ex. no. 12*

◀ Anonymous German, **Burning Books of the Alexandrian Library.** 1493. According to an old historical tradition, the Great Library at Alexandria, the Greco-Roman world's greatest repository of written knowledge, was destroyed during a siege by the forces of Julius Caesar. *Ex. no. 39*

▶ **Martin Luther's translation of the Old Testament.** 1534. *New York Public Library: Rare Books and Manuscripts.*

Ultimately, the imperial court was unable to enforce the anti-Lutheran censorship decrees of Charles V. This is evident from the frequent and ever more emphatic reissuing of regulations, sometimes even with identical texts and with the emperor referring to "my previous edict." In an edict of 1524, Charles V stated that his intent was to reinforce what he had proclaimed in the Edict of Worms only three years before, and in 1548 he complained outright that previous decrees had been ineffective. Through the Edict of Speyer, in 1570, he outlawed the operation of presses located in out-of-the-way places, which were difficult for the authorities to control, and allowed presses to operate only in free imperial cities or in towns that had a princely court or a university. Despite official disapproval, however, German pamphleteers flourished. They benefited from cheap paper, good trade routes, and the ease with which forbidden broadsheets and pamphlets could be smuggled. The authorities, by contrast, had to contend with all the impediments to effective censorship: a multitude of political jurisdictions, overburdened or easily bribed censors, conflicts between lay and ecclesiastical authorities, lax magistrates, and mutual aid among Protestant publishers, who exercised their own form of censorship in many parts of Germany by refusing to print any pro-Catholic material.

Primary among Reformation images were the portraits of Martin Luther himself; the radical new theology that he promulgated gave his image a polemical character. Lucas Cranach the Elder, Luther's close friend and frequent collaborator on polemical projects, created the prototypical Luther portraits in a group of engravings of 1520 and 1521. In 1520, Cranach engraved two different portraits of Luther, an indication of the enormous demand for his likeness only three years after his momentous proclamation of the 95 Theses. These engravings portray Luther in his ecclesiastical role, tonsured and wearing the habit of an Augustinian monk. By contrast, in the engraving of 1521, Cranach shows him in profile as a doctor of theology, wearing the hat peculiar to that rank, thus emphasizing the biblical learning so important in his epoch-making appearance before the Diet of Worms, an event which took place shortly before this engraving was made.

As the Reformer's fame spread, other artists, to whom Luther was not available to sit for his portrait, relied again and again on Cranach's engravings, but reinterpreted them in significant ways. For example, in his etched portrait of 1523 (fig. 1), Daniel Hopfer closely copied Luther's physiognomy in profile from Cranach's engraving of 1521, but also fundamentally transformed his model, giving the image a new meaning: rays of light in the form of a halo emanate from Luther's head, casting him in the guise of a saint. Such a metamorphosis was entirely contrary to Luther's own teaching on the veneration of saints, but he had no control over portraits of himself created in distant parts of Germany. Moreover, the saintly visage effectively conformed to the expectations of potential buyers, accustomed to the image traditions of late medieval piety. Luther probably would have approved of the strategy of expressing new ideas in old forms familiar to the common person. Luther's own attempt to render the new religion accessible to his fellow Germans—evident in his Bible translations and in his many writings in the vernacular—is reflected in the use of German in the etching's inscription, another departure from the Cranach prototype. Hopfer's distich *(Des lutters gestalt mag wol verderbenn/ Sein cristlich gemiet wirt nymer sterben M.D.X.X.III.)*, in contrasting the ephemeral nature of physical appearance with the immortality of the soul, adapts a familiar Renaissance conceit about the transitoriness of worldly things. Hopfer's etching and other prints like it, such as a woodcut by Hans Sebald Beham (fig. 2), were sure to offend the Catholic faction profoundly. Indeed, the papal nuncio Aleander reported in 1521 that he had observed common folk in Worms buying and kissing such prints, and angrily denounced all images of the "holy" Luther.

Like Hopfer's etching, Beham's woodcut also shows Luther in profile, surrounded by the rays of a halo, but it expands the concept of the saintly Luther through its comparison of him with an evangelist. By placing the nimbed Luther at his desk, at work while the dove of the Holy Spirit hovers above, Beham gives the Reformer all the trappings of an inspired man of God and thereby characterizes his writings as divine revelation. The woodcut, first published as a book illustration in Nuremberg in 1520, was used again, significantly enough, as the title-page illustration of Luther's edition of the New Testament, published in Nuremberg by Hans Hergot in 1524-26. The implication that this new translation was divinely inspired could hardly have been more obvious. Beham's woodcut may have been the print that the Nuremberg city council tried to censor in 1522 when it banned the sale of all portraits of Luther accompanied by the dove. Many such images by other artists are known, however, for instance, a woodcut by Hans Baldung Grien. Several years later, in 1524, during a period of crisis, the city council felt compelled to censor all images of Luther.

A final example of the proliferation of the standardized printed portraits of Luther based on the likeness supplied by Cranach is the small

◀◀ Daniel Hopfer, **Portrait of Martin Luther.** (fig. 1) 1523. Etching. *Ex. no. 40*

◀ Hans Sebald Beham, **Portrait of Luther as Evangelist.** (fig. 2) 1520. Woodcut. *West Berlin, Staatliche Museen Preussischer Kulturbesitz.*

Des lutters gestalt mag wol verderbenn
Sein cristlich gemiet wirt nymer sterben
M·D·XXIII· D· H

engraving by Albrecht Altdorfer (fig. 3). Less polemical and more commemorative in nature, this print shows Luther's profile in a tondo or circle, recalling the tradition of Renaissance portrait medals. Only about a third as large as the etching by Hopfer, and having a border of decorative foliage rather than polemical commentary, the image has the quality of a finely wrought memento of the type Renaissance humanists were fond of exchanging among themselves.

Altdorfer's intimate portrayal remains exceptional in the generally more polemical focus of sixteenth-century Luther portraits. By contrast, the characterization of the Reformer as saint, used by Beham in the 1520s, gained in appeal as one of the major paradigms of Lutheran propaganda. During the latter half of the century, this concept was elaborated upon in prints such as *Luther in His Study* by the Master W.S. (Wolfgang Stuber?), which compares Luther to one of the fathers of the church (fig. 4). The work is a reversed and substantially smaller copy of Albrecht Dürer's masterful engraving of 1514 representing St. Jerome engrossed in scholarly work at his desk (fig. 5). The engraving's polemical content is expressed through the interplay between Luther's work shown in the image and its ominous implications for the papacy, as stated in the Latin inscription: "In life I was a plague to you, O Pope, in dying I will be your death." Master W.S. emphasizes the significance of Luther's activity as a scholar and translator of the Bible, which puts the true word of God at the disposal

▲ Albrecht Altdorfer, **Martin Luther.** (fig. 3) After 1521. Engraving. *Ex. no. 41*

▶ Wolfgang Stuber? **Luther in His Study.** (fig. 4) Late sixteenth century. Engraving. *Ex. no. 47*

of all Christians and thus reveals the false doctrines of the pope. Both the stylistic evidence and the reference to Luther's death in the inscription suggest that the engraving was made well after Luther died in 1546. Master W.S. probably borrowed Dürer's well-known composition because St. Jerome, like Luther, had produced a famous Bible translation, but the artist, working around 1470-80, seems to have been unaware of the historical irony of his choice. Of all four fathers of the church, St. Jerome was the one Luther disliked most, as is evident from numerous remarks in the *Table Talk*, and from Luther's *Commentary on Galatians* of 1535, throughout which he makes disparaging observations on the errors in St. Jerome's much earlier commentary on the same biblical text. Luther's aversion to St. Jerome was probably reinforced by the latter's inordinate fondness of relics, monasticism, and other practices of the medieval church, and perhaps by the fact that Erasmus so admired St. Jerome. With equal inappropriateness, Master W.S. retains the Catholic paraphernalia that hang from the wall of St. Jerome's study in the Dürer print—a rosary and a cardinal's hat.

The Catholic clergy's neglect to practice what it preached was a frequent theme of Protestant propaganda. One of the artistically most accomplished expressions of this criticism during the Reformation appeared in the series of 41 small woodcuts, usually called the *Dance of Death*, created by Hans Holbein the Younger. Holbein's designs were finished and

▲ Albrecht Dürer, **St. Philip.** 1526. Engraving. *Ex. no. 49*

◄ Albrecht Dürer, **St. Jerome in His Study.** (fig. 5) 1514. Engraving. *Ex. no. 48*

Hans Holbein the Younger, **The Nun.**
(fig. 6) 1538. Woodcut from the *Dance of
Death. National Gallery of Art,
Rosenwald Collection.*

cut into the woodblocks by the exceptionally gifted woodcutter Hans Lützelberger in about 1525, but although some trial proofs were made then, the complete series was not published until 1538, possibly owing to censorship restrictions or the publisher's fear of reprisals. In his depiction of death coming to fetch a nun (fig. 6), Holbein castigates the licentiousness that existed in some Catholic religious orders. The nun, kneeling before her private altar, and supposedly occupied with her devotions, is in fact far more interested in the charming young man who strums a lute while seated on her bed. The intimate locale and the act of playing a lute convey the unambiguously erotic meaning of the woodcut, for in sixteenth-century German slang, lute-playing was a euphemism for love-making. The implications of such lascivious conduct for the nun's salvation are expressed through the haggard female figure of death, who reaches to extinguish the candle, symbol of the immortal soul. The hourglass toppled in the foreground indicates that time has run out for the nun. In 1526, Luther proposed his own solution to the problem of sexual desire among monks and nuns in *Das Babstum* (fig. 10), a polemical tract discussed below.

In addition to hagiographic imagery as employed by Beham and Master W.S., or the theme of the dance of death illustrated by Holbein, Reformation publicists frequently chose biblical themes to demonstrate how their opponents subverted God's will. The parable of the Good Shepherd, for example, a favorite motif, was used effectively to elicit the viewer's sympathy with the innocent flock of Christ, menaced by ravaging wolves. An illustrated broadsheet issued about 1521 shows the flock gathered for protection around the crucified Christ, while two wolves wearing a papal tiara and a cardinal's hat devour them one by one. But the imagery of the hierarchy as wolves who prey on the flock fed the propaganda mills of both camps. Indeed, a German engraving issued by the Catholic faction casts Martin Luther in the role of the wolf in monk's clothing (fig. 7), his hands uplifted in a mock-pious gesture of prayer but his furry legs revealing his true nature. Scattered around him are the bones, dismembered limbs, and carcasses of his prey. Luther's ravenous appetite is shown to be inspired by the devil, who transmits evil intentions by blowing them—akin to whispering—into his ear through a long, thin horn. Here the anonymous artist illustrates the devil as "ear blower" *(Ohrenbläser),* so familiar in sixteenth-century German folklore. The engraving is replete with references to biblical passages; those at the upper left were meant as pointed commentaries on the turmoil Luther created within the church and the errors of his theology. The reference to Philippians is an exhortation to the Christian duties of harmony, humility, and service to the faith, which it is implied Luther took no heed of. In Psalm 4, God laments that sinners turn his glory into shame, and love only vanity. Job says God is misrepresented by "forgers of lies" and warns that no hypocrites will prevail before God. The passage from Jude warns against "ungodly men who crept in unawares, turning the grace of God into lasciviousness" and foretells the imminent destruction of unbelievers. Whereas these biblical references are all directed against the false prophet Luther, those on the lower part of the sheet express the cry of the persecuted flock, as in Psalm 13: "How long wilt thou forget me, O Lord? How long shall my enemy be exalted over me?"

The wolf in monk's clothing actually predates the Reformation as an anti-clerical polemical motif. For example, in an anonymous allegorical woodcut professing Hussite views, made in Germany during the third quarter of the fifteenth century, a wolf appears in the habit of a Dominican

PHILIP · 2 · PSAL · 4 ·

IOB · 13 ·

IVDE · A ·

AGGEI · I ·

· PSALM · 13 ·

◄   Anonymous
German? **Luther as a
Wolf in the Fold** or
**Luther as a Wolf in
Monk's Clothing.** (fig. 7)
First half of sixteenth
century. Engraving.
Ex. no. 43

monk, while a fox wears the papal tiara. Evidently when attacks on the flock were to be suggested, wolves and foxes served the polemical purpose equally well. This was surely the reason why, in 1524, the Nuremberg city council censored a mural on a burgher's house that showed the pope as a fox wearing the papal tiara. The councillors demanded that the tiara be removed to eliminate all reference to the pope.

Another instance of a biblical parable used polemically, to show how the opposing camp makes a mockery of God's will, illustrates the story of

Evangelium Lucæ am xvi Cap.

Hie sihstu leser lobesann	So in allem wollust gelebt	Bekomen vons reichn schlemers tisch	Der reiche man darnach auch starb	Gelebt vnd in mancher gefahr	Darumb man sie sollen sterben
Den heilgen papst vnd frommen man	Nach lust vnd freud alzeit gestrebt	Vil weniger auch gebrathene fisch	Zu seinem grab die hell erwarb,	Hat ausgestanden ihnnmerdar,	Die hell Zu ihrem theil ererben
Wie er vnd sein gantz hofgesind	Darggen der arme lazarus	Auch endlich in solcher armuht	Darin er brenend immer ligt	Vom papst vnd seiner gantze roch	Darin sie bleiben allezeit
So gar verfressene brüder seind	In seinem leben darben muss	Sein lebn dem herrn ergehen thut,	Kein tröpfflein wasser in erquick	DarZu erlitten hohn vnd spott,	Kein trost mehr ist in ewigkeit
Drumb billich man vergleiche sie	Vnd kondt auch nicht die brösamlein	Vnd ward in abrahams schof tragn	Also wirde auch der luther werdt	Nach seinem todt er itzund ist,	Nach dem man hie gelebt hat
Dem reichen man den schlemer hie	Darmit Zustilln den hunger sein	Alda ein endt hat all sein Clagen	Weil er all hie auff diser erdt,	In ewige freude vnd won Zur frist,	Belohnt sie got auch mirder that

the rich man and the poor Lazarus from the Gospel of St. Luke (fig. 8). This broadsheet of about 1562, consisting of an engraving and six stanzas of explanatory text, condemns the worldly pursuits of the pope and his courtiers, a favorite theme of Reformation publicists. By comparing the pope's lavish lifestyle to that of the rich man in the parable, the anonymous artist gives biblical sanction to the retribution visited upon the pope, who is shown burning in hell in the right background. The engraving offers a detailed display of papist vices: the pope kisses a nun, who suggestively holds the hand of the cardinal next to her, who in turn is singing and gesticulating wildly. Behind him a donkey in a monk's habit, signifying folly, brandishes a fox's tail like a flyswatter, a reference to flattery. A canon and a bishop seated opposite each other at a table are drinking merrily, while two monks vomiting and falling down in a stupor demonstrate the results of excessive indulgence in food and drink. The gesture of a third monk, in the foreground, pouring wine from one vessel into another, is an ironic reference to the virtue of temperance. A second monk approaches carrying yet another wine jug, while two more wine vessels stand chilled in a vat of cool water. The bread and wine on the altar in the foreground are being put to purely secular use, showing how the clergy make a travesty of their liturgical duties. Instead of proclaiming the Gospel, a monk brings on a backgammon board with a small case containing the pieces needed to play. In the left foreground two musicians serenade the revellers on fife and drum, while in the right background canons in full priestly regalia approach bearing the next courses of the banquet. But the demonic nature of the revellers is revealed not only through their misdeeds but through their monstrous appearance. The deformities caused by sin are expressed through the same symbolic device used in the previously mentioned satire on Luther (fig. 7): the legs on the fife-player, drummer, and guardsmen in the background terminate in cleft hooves and bird's claws.

Contrasting starkly to the debauched clerics, Luther, in the guise of the poor Lazarus, sits humbly on a pile of hay and points admonishingly to the Scriptures. The dog licking his sores, mentioned in the biblical text, offers Luther more Christian charity than the menacing prelate, whose attack, however, the long-suffering outcast ignores. The artist, more fully to exploit the polemical potential of the biblical story, has altered its original emphasis. Whereas the Gospel of St. Luke dwells primarily on the eternal

◄   Anonymous German broadsheet. **The Pope as a Rich Man at Table.** (fig. 8) Ca. 1562. Engraving. *Ex. no. 44*

▶   Georg Pencz, **The Rich Man in Hell and Lazarus in Heaven.** Ca. 1542-43. Engraving. *Ex. no. 45*

reward of the protagonists—the rich man burning in hell while Lazarus is being rocked in the bosom of Abraham—the engraving achieves its polemic by focusing on the sinful earthly existence of the rich-man/pope. Indeed, the moral indictment is so scathing that the broadsheet was banned by the censors; a bookseller is known to have suffered torture and imprisonment several times for having sold it. The censors were unable, however, to prevent the printing of further editions.

Reformation propaganda is full of vitriolic diatribes attacking papist self-indulgence and neglect of priestly functions, but the special effectiveness of this broadsheet lies in its skill in marshaling the word of God to its own cause. This polemical tactic and numerous details of the image place the broadsheet in a specific tradition, engendered by the *Passional Christi und Antichristi* (fig. 9), one of the earliest and most famous antipapal polemical tracts, whose publication Luther personally supervised. First printed in Wittenberg in 1521, with illustrations by Lucas Cranach the Elder and several workshop assistants, the *Passional* compares the exemplary life of Christ with the self-serving life of the pope (characterized as Antichrist) and the papal curia. In a series of thirteen antithetical pairs of woodcuts, each page-opening juxtaposes an episode from Christ's ministry, on the left, with a papal practice, on the right, that is suggested to be diametrically opposed to Christ's teaching. The polemic is driven home in each instance by the text under the woodcuts, cleverly selected to emphasize Christ's devotion to his mission and to his followers on the one hand versus the institutionalized neglect of parishioners by the Catholic hierarchy on the other. The seventh pair of images, for example, shows Christ on the left preaching to the multitude; in the biblical passage below he expresses his profound commitment to preaching about his Father's kingdom (Luke 4:43-44). By contrast, on the right, the pope presides at a lavish meal with a bishop, a canon, and a monk, while the text below ironically describes the overworked bishops as being too busy with their political affairs to preach God's word and as gluttonous "animals" devoted only to

▼ Lucas Cranach, **Passional Christi und Antichristi.** (fig. 9) 1521. Woodcuts. *Ex. no. 8*

only to living well (Isaiah 56:12). The pope and his entourage, seated gorging themselves in regal splendor under a canopy, waited upon by servants who carry three dishes at a time, and listening to a serenade by musicians, are all motifs that recur in the later broadsheet (fig. 8), where, in similar fashion, the juxtaposition with Luther pointing to his Bible (rather than with Christ himself) draws attention to the papists' neglect of their duty to proclaim God's word.

The *Passional* was the first full-blown polemical tract issued by the Lutheran camp in Wittenberg; the images actually carry far more polemical weight than the brief texts printed below them. Philipp Melanchthon and Johann Schwertfeger chose the texts from the Bible and from papal decretals for the ironical commentary they add to each corresponding woodcut. The brief ten-line epilogue that appears instead of a colophon was perhaps written by Luther himself. The originators of the project were conscious of the inflammatory nature of the *Passional*, which does not enumerate the compilers of the texts and carries neither the place of publication nor the name of the printer. The first edition of the pamphlet was issued shortly after the Diet of Worms, whose strict censorship regulations were reason enough to prefer anonymity. Nevertheless, the epilogue specifically addresses the potential objections of the censors and offers its own rationale of why the pamphlet should not be considered libellous: everything it cites is not only accepted practice among the papists but is even set forth in canon law. The Wittenberg reformers astutely used the age-old polemical technique of turning their opponents' own words against them. The appearance of several new editions in German and one in Latin during the second half of 1521 alone suggests the pamphlet's enormous popularity.

Another anonymous tract disseminated from Wittenberg is *The Papacy and Its Members (Das Babstum mit seynen gliedern gemalet und beschryben)*, an illustrated catalogue describing the Catholic hierarchy and criticizing the proliferation of monastic orders and their godless ways.

◀ **Das Babstum mit seynen gliedern gemalet und beschryben gebessert und gemehrt.** (fig. 10) 1526. *Ex. no. 10*

As in the *Passional,* Luther was directly involved in the publication, whose preface and epilogue he wrote; again the artists of Cranach's workshop collaborated. Issued in 1526 both as a pamphlet and a broadsheet, the tract was illustrated with 57 woodcuts of representatives of the church.

Luther's diatribe against monasticism must be understood in light of contemporary events: the tract was issued the year following Luther's marriage to the former nun Katharina von Bora, a union demonstratively intended as Luther's answer to monasticism. In the preface Luther notes the utter failure of Catholic attempts to impose sexual abstinence on monks, nuns, and clerics, and repeats his view that they should marry. The edition of the pamphlet exhibited here (fig. 10) is actually an expanded one *(gebessert und gemehrt),* published in Nuremberg during the same year, which contains Luther's texts set in verses and illustrations by Hans Sebald Beham, based on the Cranach woodcuts but somewhat simplified. Unlike the *Passional,* the texts rather than the images convey the polemical message, but the woodcuts effectively emphasize the sheer number of monastic orders that are ridiculed: the Beham version has no less than 74 illustrations of clerics. In the epilogue Luther again takes up the issue of censorship, asserting that the tract is not libellous but merely calls attention to the public offenses of the Catholics and thus is doing God's will.

Perhaps the most interesting and best documented instance of the censorship of antipapal polemics in Reformation Germany occurred with the publication of *A Wondrous Prophecy of the Papacy (Eyn wunderliche Weyssagung von dem Babstum)* in Nuremberg in 1527 (fig. 11). The pamphlet consists of thirty allegorical woodcuts by Erhard Schön illustrating the history and ultimate defeat of the papacy, accompanied by brief explanations of the images by Andreas Osiander, the Lutheran preacher at St. Lawrence's, and by two rhyming couplets per image, penned by the poet Hans Sachs. The *Wondrous Prophecy* is based on a much older prophetic source, the *Vaticinia de summis pontificibus,* attributed to the medieval sectarian Joachim of Fiore and to a certain bishop "Anselmus," which Osiander had come across in a Bolognese edition of 1515, in the library of the Carthusian monastery in Nuremberg, and

▶ Erhard Schön, **Eyn Wunderliche Weyssagung von dem Babstum.** (fig. 11) 1527. *Humanities Research Center, The University of Texas at Austin.*

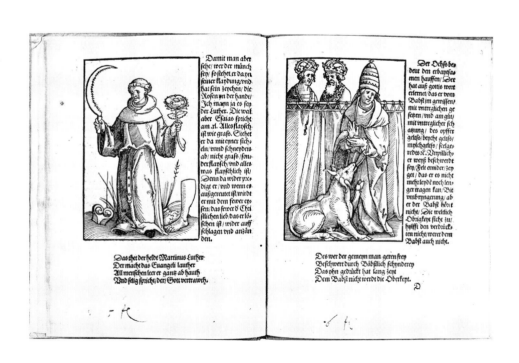

which served his polemical ends as evidence that generations well before Luther had foretold the increasing sinfulness and impending demise of the papacy. Distrusting what he considered a heavily edited text in the Italian edition, and suspecting that it obscured the full extent of the original author's criticism of the medieval church, Osiander simply deleted it and composed his own to elucidate the images. Interestingly enough, Osiander trusted the authenticity of the pictures in his Bolognese edition far more than the text, so he took over into his version only the woodcuts, copied by Erhard Schön with minimal changes.

Following in the tradition of the *Passional*, Osiander equates the pope with Antichrist, dwells at length on his worldly concerns and misuse of authority as a temporal lord and warmonger, and then tries to show that all these ills prophesied as early as the thirteenth century were fulfilled in historical fact. Finally, the last five images with their texts foretell the pope's eventual unmasking and loss of power, which will be returned to the true servants of God until Judgment Day. To achieve the necessary topical relevance, Osiander and Schön take a few liberties with their prototype. For instance, Luther himself appears among the opposition to the pope (fig. 11). He is shown as an Augustinian monk, holding his heraldic emblem, the rose, and a sickle with which he will mow down the flesh, symbolized by the severed foot, a reference to Isaiah 40:6. The branding iron at the left Luther will use to rekindle the fire of Christian love, which Osiander suggests the pope has allowed to die. Other topical references are made to religious politics of the time, such as the Diet of Worms, where the pope managed to prevail with the assistance of his armies, and two later diets held at Nuremberg, where God's word triumphed, as the Recesses from these gatherings demonstrate.

Osiander's pseudo-rehabilitation of a medieval prognostic to give prophetic legitimacy to his personal arguments was a common tactic during the Reformation. Among the earlier examples is a pamphlet edited by Ulrich von Hutten, based on a medieval text critical of Henry IV and Pope Gregory VII, annotated with Hutten's own antipapal rhetoric and published in Mainz by Johann Schöffer. Pope Leo X complained bitterly about Hutten's pamphlet to Archbishop Albrecht von Brandenburg, who ordered the printer apprehended and sale of the pamphlet suspended. Likewise, in Nuremberg, the town councillors felt Osiander's pictorial prophecy was far too inflammatory during a period when they were attempting to steady the city's precarious relations with the emperor. The tract, they explained, was sure to offend and embitter common folk and would have no positive effect on the community. After reprimanding the participants in the project for not having cleared their tract with the censors before publication, as required by law, the councillors censored the *Wondrous Prophecy*, confiscated the 600 copies remaining at Guldenmund's printing shop, forbade Osiander from publishing any of his writings without their prior consent, and advised Hans Sachs to cultivate his shoemaker's trade instead of composing provocative verses. Alleged financial hardship persuaded the councillors to compensate Guldenmund for his loss in sales with 12 florins, to return the confiscated woodblocks (since the images were merely copies of the Italian ones), and to permit Osiander to print the Bolognese edition's text if he so desired. In this case, the councillors were not exercising their censorship rights solely for the public record to ease relations with the emperor; in the archival documents they seem genuinely intent on taking Osiander's tract out of circulation. Possibly its allusions to the delicate issue of the diets at Worms and Nuremberg alarmed them. They even wrote to Frankfurt asking their colleagues there to look out for the *Wondrous Prophecy* at the annual book fairs and to buy up and send to Nuremberg at the council's expense any copies found in circulation.

Perhaps the most extensively studied instance of an antipapal broadsheet that was censored by the Nuremberg town council is the *Papal Coat of Arms* (fig. 12). Here again the polemical strategy is to give the pope himself full responsibility for his own demise. The heraldic image, normally used to assemble the bearer's honors and insignia of office, has been subverted here to become an accusatory litany of the pope's misuse of office. The papal shield, surmounted by the tiara, is supported by the shafts of the two crossed keys of St. Peter, the shattered parts of which lie scattered about, signs that the pope's power has been destroyed. The keys serve as the gallows from which two victims dangle, the pope and Judas. On the analogy of the thirty pieces of silver for which Judas betrayed Christ, four large money bags appear in the central shield. The implication of the image, reinforced by the text, is that the pope is not, as he claims, the heir of St. Peter but rather of Judas. The pope's means of implementing his greed are suggested by the bishops' mitres, royal crowns, and cardinal's hat protruding from the money bags—headdresses which signify the henchmen who help the pope fill his purse. The corresponding text describes a fictitious Judgment scene in which the pope appears before Christ. St. Peter, acting as prosecutor, enumerates the crimes of the pope, who then receives a place in hell next to Satan. In addition to the report of its censorship in Nuremberg, the broadsheet is mentioned in other contemporary commentaries that have survived, both by Luther himself, who characterizes it as just retribution for the banning (another misuse of papal power), and declares he will "hang the pope on his own keys," and by Johannes Cochlaeus, of the Catholic camp, who vented his rage over the broadsheet in a letter of 1538. In fact, Luther did not "hang the pope on his own keys": the polemic bites so deeply precisely because Luther's text and the analogy to the suicide of Judas show that the Pope himself, realizing his betrayal of Christ, has taken his own life.

By mid-century, the Lutheran religion had become firmly entrenched in many parts of Europe. Despite some military victories, the Catholic forces were fighting a losing battle, and Catholic censorship sometimes had a counterproductive effect. For example, Luther's hymn "Preserve Us Lord with Your Word" (ca. 1542)—roughly the Lutheran equivalent of the "Internationale"—was republished by Pancratius Kempff in Magdeburg

▼ Cranach Workshop, **The Papal Coat of Arms.** (fig. 12) Sixteenth century. Woodcut. *Kunstsammlungen der Veste Coburg.*

▼ ► Martin Luther, **Preserve Us Lord with Your Word.** (fig. 13) Nineteenth-century reprint after an original broadsheet in Wolfenbüttel. Ca. 1550. *Staatsbibliothek, Berlin.*

around 1550 (fig. 13), specifically because its lyrics had been banned in most other parts of Germany. Long angered by Luther's lyrics, the Catholics were able to forbid the singing of the hymn during the Interim, the religious settlement imposed on the Protestant territories following their defeat in the First Schmalkaldic War in 1547. Even the Protestants, in some cities, censored the first stanza, to avoid giving an excuse for further Catholic attacks. They replaced Luther's accusation, that the pope and the Turks were attempting to overthrow Christ from his throne, with a neutral reference to the devil. The woodcut (fig. 13) illustrates the futility of the pope's tactics. Christ the Judge sits enthroned in heaven while a Turk, the pope, and the Catholic clergy are sent to perdition. On both sides, the evangelical witnesses to the pope's demise are assembled: at the left, Luther, composer of the first three stanzas printed below, is shown pointing to the triumphant Christ. As the leader of the reformers, among them Melanchthon and Jan Hus, Luther appears with John Frederick the Magnanimous, Elector of Saxony (second from left), who was still the emperor's captive when this broadsheet was published. At the right, various ladies of the house of Saxony are gathered, including Sibylla of Cleves, John Frederick's spouse, as well as Katharina von Bora, Luther's wife. The New York Public Library owns an edition of Lutheran hymns—*Geystliche Lieder*, published before the Interim by Valentin Babst in Leipzig in 1545—in which Luther's original first stanza appears. Later editions often have the "expurgated" text instead, depending upon the political circumstances of the time and place of publication.

SOURCES

The best and most recent studies on polemical prints of the German Reformation are: Robert W. Scribner, *For the Sake of Simple Folk: Popular Propaganda for the German Reformation* (Cambridge: Cambridge University Press, 1981), and Konrad Hoffmann's section (pp. 219-254) of the catalogue accompanying the exhibition *Martin Luther und die Reformation in Deutschland*, held at the Germanisches Nationalmuseum in Nuremberg in the summer of 1983. From the same museum an exhibition catalogue of 1979, *Reformation in Nürnberg, Umbruch und Bewahrung: 1490–1580*, adds additional material. Another exhibition catalogue, *Illustrierte Flugblätter aus den Jahrhunderten der Reformation und der Glaubenskämpfe*, Wolfgang Harms and Beate Rattay, eds. (1983), provides a useful study of the broadsheets in the collection of the Kunstsammlungen der Veste Coburg. More general sources on broadsheets, including some polemical examples, are: Wolfgang Brückner, *Populäre Druckgraphik Europas: Deutschland, vom 15. bis zum 20. Jahrhundert* (Munich: Callwey, 1969); H. Meuche and I. Neumeister, eds., *Flugblätter der Reformation und des Bauernkrieges, 50 Blätter aus der Sammlung des Schloss-museums Gotha*, 2 vols. (Leipzig: Insel, 1976); and W. Harms, M. Schilling and A. Wang, eds., *Deutsche Illustrierte Flugblätter des 16. und 17. Jahrhunderts. Vol. 2, Die Sammlung der Herzog August Bibliothek in Wolfenbüttel, 2: Historica* (Munich: Kraus, 1980). The most reliable and informative studies of censorship during this period in Germany are: Arndt Müller, "Die Zensurpolitik der Reichsstadt Nürnberg von der Einführung der Buchdruckerkunst bis zum Ende der Reichsstadtzeit" (*Mitteilungen des Vereins für Geschichte der Stadt Nürnberg*, vol. 49, 1959, pp. 66-169); Ulrich Eisenhardt, *Die kaiserliche Aufsicht über Buchdruck, Buchhandel und Presse im Heiligen Römischen Reich Deutscher Nation (1496–1806)*, in the series *Studien und Quellen zur Geschichte des deutschen Verfassungsrechts*, Vol. 3 (Karlsruhe: C. F. Müller, 1970); Karl Schottenloher, "Beschlagnahmte Druckschriften aus der Frühzeit der Reformation" (*Zeitschrift für Bücherfreunde*, Neue Folge, vol. 8, part 2, 1917, pp. 305-321); and G. Costa, "Die Rechtseinrichtung der Zensur in der Reichsstadt Augsburg" (*Zeitschrift des historischen Vereins für Schwaben und Neuburg*, vol. 42, 1916, pp. 1-82). The finest article specifically about satirical imagery in the Reformation is Konrad Hoffmann, "Typologie, Exemplarik und reformatorische Bildsatire," in *Kontinuität und Umbruch* [*Tübinger Beiträge zur Geschichtsforschung*, Vol. 2] ed. Josef Nolte (Tübingen: Klett Cotta, 1978), pp. 189-210.

4

A
New Consensus
1600–1700

M A R G A R E T   C.   J A C O B

In 1600 in an open field near St. Peter's Square in Rome, Giordano Bruno was burned to death by the Inquisition. He met his tragic fate because he had spoken at the courts, the universities, and the aristocratic homes of Europe about the necessity of finding an alternative religion to Reformation Protestantism and Counter-Reformation Catholicism. He had sought to use the new heliocentric science of Copernicus to instill the worship of nature itself, as well as nature's God, as the sole basis of religious belief, and he did not shrink from magic and mysticism as ways of exploring this newly discovered, all-embracing, sun-centered natural world. In ten major books he published his beliefs; he gloried in Copernican heliocentricity and he ridiculed the clergy, both Protestant and Catholic; he identified with the old pagan gods and he advocated sexual liberty. In short, he challenged all the religious beliefs and social mores held dear by the legally established churches and the aristocrats who supported them.

Just short of one hundred years later, an English freethinker and follower of Bruno, John Toland, published a book, *Christianity Not Mysterious* (1696), that proclaimed all the Christian mysteries, for example, the Trinity and transubstantiation, as so much nonsense. A grand jury in London condemned the book, not its author, but was unable to prevent copies of it being freely circulated. Many copies of the book survive today; by contrast, copies of Bruno's books are exceedingly rare, the Inquisition having destroyed every one it could find. Clearly, a dramatic change in the practice of censorship, and therefore in the values and beliefs of the groups who made those laws, had occurred between 1600 and 1700.

It is well known that in parts of seventeenth-century Europe, particularly in northern and western countries and cities, the literate social elites grew more tolerant of certain outrageous ideas appearing in print. In Paris during the 1650s, for example, some French aristocrats allowed their homes to become the scenes of learned gatherings where skepticism about the teachings of the church could be openly expressed. In atten-

MARGARET C. JACOB, a founding member of The Institute for Research in History, is currently on a fellowship from the National Science Foundation and a guest of the Science Dynamics Department of the University of Amsterdam. Her most recent book, *The Radical Enlightenment: Pantheists, Freemasons and Republicans,* appeared in 1981 (Boston: George Allen & Unwin). She is currently at work on a study of the integration of science and Western culture.

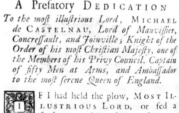

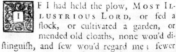

dance at such gatherings was the freethinker Cyrano de Bergerac, made famous by a satirical play that focused on his nose (which was almost certainly quite normal), but rightly to be remembered as one of the first thinkers, after Bruno, to speculate on the possibility of life on other planets. In a work entitled *The States and Empires of the Moon* (1656), Cyrano also speculated on the possibility that the earth itself was eternal. That was a pagan form of naturalism, regarded by the church as an especially outrageous type of heresy.

In those same circles various heretical manuscripts were also circulated, so outrageous in their content that they simply could not be published. One such long Latin manuscript was called *Theophrastus redivivus*, named after an ancient Greek follower of Aristotle, but largely concerned with the idea that nature alone was the source of all life and motion in the universe. It also claimed that Jesus, Moses, and Mohammed had been impostors. It was not until the early eighteenth century that a circle of freethinkers and publishers in The Netherlands were able to bring out a book that popularized that idea and proclaimed that nature alone is what Christians have chosen to call God. That text became known in the eighteenth century as the *Treatise on the Three Impostors*, first published in an extremely rare edition of 1719. Its publication alone indicates that by the early eighteenth century the press, at least in Holland, had become very difficult to control, or more precisely, that the authorities were less interested by that time in trying to control it.

But why had these changes occurred, and why in some places and not in others? We may assume that human beings grow more tolerant when they feel less fundamentally threatened by certain ideas or their advocates. We can be skeptical or admit probability, rather than demand absolute certainty, on some matters, only when we are sure about others. The new confidence in some matters found among educated elites, particularly in England, The Netherlands, Switzerland, and the independent German cities—that is, in the publishing centers, the free presses of the

▼ **Index of Prohibited Books.** 1664. This edition lists works by such writers as Pascal, Galileo, and Kepler. *Ex. no. 58*

◄◄ John Toland, **On the Nature, Place, and Time of Death of Jordano Bruno** and Bruno's **On the Infinite Universe and Worlds.** 1726. Bruno was burned for heresy in 1600 along with most early editions of his work. This is Toland's tribute to Bruno and translation of his work. *Ex. no. 59*

◄ John Toland, **Christianity Not Mysterious; or a Treatise Shewing, That There Is Nothing in the Gospel Contrary to Reason Nor above It.** 1696. Although condemned as blasphemous by a London jury, Toland's treatise circulated widely. *New York Public Library: Annex.*

► Savinien de Cyrano de Bergerac, **The Comical History of the States and Empires of the Worlds of the Moon and Sun.** 1687. *Ex. no. 79*

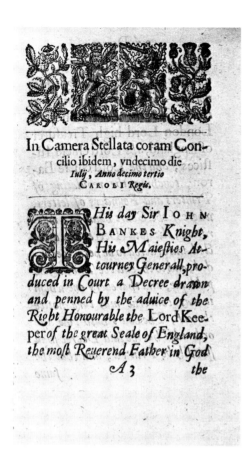

In Camera Stellata coram Con-
cilio ibidem, vndecimo die
Iulij, Anno decimo tertio
CAROLI Regis.

His day Sir IOHN
BANKES Knight,
His Maiesties At-
tourney Generall, pro-
duced in Court a Decree drawn
and penned by the aduice of the
Right Honourable the Lord Keeper of the great Seale of England,
the most Reuerend Father in God
A 3   the

▲ **Royal decree of 1637.** This measure
extended the licensing laws to new types of
books that began appearing in the wake of the
expansion of the book trade. *Ex no. 61*

late seventeenth century—derived from a variety of sources, all of them important in the history of the abolition of censorship.

The aristocratic circles of mid-seventeenth-century Paris that permitted Cyrano de Bergerac to speak openly never sought to change the actual relationship between publishing and censorship within the French kingdom. They were content to discuss their ideas in private, and by the 1680s did nothing to stop the monopoly which Louis XIV and the church exercised over the presses. The central policy that insured that monopoly demanded that every book be submitted for review before publication. In addition the government did everything in its power to drive small presses out of business. The logic of that policy lay in the assumption that fewer presses were easier to control, and not surprisingly the policy worked. French absolutism demanded absolute loyalty to the state as the only alternative to the political chaos that had gripped France during the sixteenth century. At that time Protestants and Catholics had engaged in a bitter civil war that threatened the very survival of monarchy itself. The French elites of the seventeenth century gave their support to an absolute monarch, and hence to censorship, because by and large they preferred to maintain that central power as the major guarantor of their own power.

By the late seventeenth century, in places where we find freer presses than those in France, we are able to observe the emergence of new social systems that permitted elites to maintain their power within their communities without necessarily relying on the institution of absolute monarchy and the control it exercised over all forms of public expression. Most of those elites were in Protestant countries. Protestant culture demanded the establishment of a consensus within a congregation generally led by older, wealthy men from the community. Authority within the church, and hence in society, rested not on the power of bishops appointed by the king and responsible to him, such as we find in Catholic countries, but on the authority of powerful laymen within their congregations.

Individuals who disagreed with such men might not be any better off than they would be if they disagreed with the local priest or bishop, but the effect upon the printing presses was palpable. Where we find wealthy merchants or businessmen comfortably in control of their local churches, or eager to maintain their position within the Protestant churches against the claims to authority of the Protestant clergy, there we generally find printing presses less censored, and hence more free. For example, magistrates in the Dutch cities of the late seventeenth century frequently refused to close down printing presses that offended local Calvinists, in particular the clergy, because they enjoyed seeing the clergy's ideas challenged in print, or because they enjoyed having access to new ideas, or because they needed the taxes collected from the printing firms. This does not mean that they were less devout as Christians, but rather that they were sufficiently secure in their communities to permit a wider degree of public discourse. This was the context that permitted The Hague to become one of the main publishing cities of Western Europe. The books that came from its presses, frequently published in French, the international language of the period, explored questions in politics and science that could not be discussed in print in France or Spain.

The structure of the Dutch publishing firms, the freest in Europe during the late seventeenth century, was also unique. Presses competed ruthlessly among themselves, bankruptcy always being a possibility for any firm. Nevertheless, the publishers' guild in any city was not reluctant to use its considerable political influence to secure lower taxes or to keep the clergy from exercising any direct control over the presses. Representatives of the guild held public office and socialized with the lay magistrates. In any case, most of the heretical books they published that attacked French absolutism or questioned certain aspects of Christian doctrine were in French. Had they been in Dutch the local clergy would undoubtedly have been more alarmed.

In addition, the system of Dutch government in this period was unique in that it was highly decentralized: the representative body of the Dutch Republic, the Estates General, had little direct national power. That fact, when translated into the history of publishing, means that even if a press got in trouble with the local magistrates in a particular town, all the publisher needed to do was move to the next town. Indeed many publishers maintained business ties in various towns; a book found to be offensive in Delft might easily sell in Amsterdam. It is also true that the Dutch were bitterly hostile to Louis XIV in the period after 1685. In that year France expelled its Protestant population that would not convert to Catholicism, and many of them fled to The Netherlands. From that haven French Protestant publishers printed book after book that attacked the French system. The political structure of the Dutch Republic, coupled with its growing fear that the French colossus might attempt to control or invade the Low Countries, provided the framework within which the printing presses of the Dutch cities flourished.

A similar situation in relation to the fear of absolutism obtained in England after the Revolution of 1688-89. That event, the dethronement of James II (1685-88), removed the specter of absolute monarchy from England itself, abolished the church courts with their power to police mores and beliefs, and insured *habeas corpus* and trial by jury for the propertied classes. For nearly half a century before, leading members of the gentry (who ran the counties and shires) had tried, with their allies in the towns and cities, to bring the royal government into the orbit of their power. The English Revolution (1640-60) was the first of the great modern revolutions that pitted the supporters of divine-right monarchy, aristocratic feudal privilege, and an independent clergy and church against those who would have the king rule in consultation with his parliament, preserve the independent power of the landed in their shires, and subordinate the interests of the church to lay domination. As a result of this massive confrontation between elements of the ruling classes, England experienced, almost by accident, a freedom of press unprecedented anywhere else in Europe. Quite simply, the mechanism of censorship (as of much else) broke down under the impact of civil war.

◀ William Faithorne, **John Milton.** 1670. Engraving. *Ex. no. 82*

▶ John Milton, **Areopagitica.** 1644. Published during the Civil War, *Areopagitica* is the English-speaking world's first great statement urging freedom of expression. *Ex. no. 66*

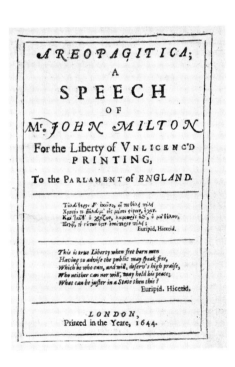

▲   Thomas Hobbes, **Leviathan.** 1651. One of the earliest Western writers to analyze the state, Hobbes also questioned the divine right of monarchs and the role of religion in society. He originated the idea of a social contract between monarch and subject. *Leviathan* was published during Cromwell's Protectorate and suppressed with the restoration of the monarchy in 1669. *Ex. no. 64*

▶   **Royal proclamation suppressing two books by John Milton** (detail). 1660. *Ex. no. 68*

The results can be seen in the publication of books by Milton, Harrington, Hobbes, and Winstanley (arguably the first "socialist"), to cite only a few, which challenged every aspect of the old order. Milton argued for the rights of couples to divorce rather than to live a life of mutual incompatibility. More important for the history of the free press, he proclaimed the necessity to end all censorship and he justified his position philosophically. Hobbes argued that the foundation of government ultimately lay in a contract of the people; it was not a gift from God. He then went on to argue that the people must set up an absolute power over themselves, but from the point of view of the divine right of kings the damage had been done. In *Leviathan* (1651) Hobbes also called the religious teachings of the clergy stories about "fairies and bugbears" and he argued that the clergy must be firmly controlled by the state. Winstanley proclaimed the land as the birthright of the common people and private property and wealth as the byproducts of an original act of thievery. James Harrington in *Oceana* (1653) laid the theoretical foundation for republican government; his ideas were widely circulated in the American colonies during the eighteenth century and used by the American revolutionaries.

Quaker pamphleteers argued for the right of every man and every woman to follow the light of God in their own hearts, while the Levellers demanded that every man, except servants, be given the vote. In 1648 an English translation of a sixteenth-century French Protestant tract, *A Vindication against Tyranny,* was published. On January 30, 1649, King Charles I of England was executed by order of parliament. The publishing freedom, though short-lived, produced works of major philosophical importance, and put forward ideas that remain to this day incompatible with censorship and tyranny.

In 1660, with the restoration of church and monarchy, censorship returned, and Milton, as a supporter of the Puritan revolution, was lucky

By the King.

A PROCLAMATION

For calling in, and suppressing of two Books written by *John Milton*; the one Intituled, *Johannis Miltoni Angli pro Populo Anglicano Defensio, contra Claudii Anonymi aliàs Salmasii, Defensionem Regiam*; and the other in answer to a Book Intituled, *The Pourtraicture of his Sacred Majesty in his Solitude and Sufferings.* And also a third Book Intituled, *The Obstructors of Justice,* written by *John Goodwin.*

CHARLES R.

Whereas John Milton, late of Westminster, in the County of Middlesex, hath Published in Print two several Books, The one Intituled, Johannis Miltoni Angli pro Populo Anglicano Defensio, contra Claudii Anonymi, aliàs Salmasii, Defensionem Regiam. And the other in Answer to a Book Intituled, The Pourtraicture of his Sacred Majesty in his Solitude and Sufferings. In both which are contained sundry Treasonable Passages against Us and Our Government, and most Impious endeavors to justifie the horrid and unmatchable Murther of Our late Dear Father, of Glorious Memory. And Whereas John Goodwin, late of Coleman-Street, London, Clerk, hath also published in Print, a Book Intituled, The Obstructors of Justice, written in defence of the traiterous Sentence against his said late Majesty. And Whereas the said John Mil

to be permitted to live out his final years at home and not in prison. Yet the ferment of the revolution had produced a transformation within English elite culture. Landed aristocrats found it increasingly beneficial to ally with men of commerce, in both the political and economic spheres. Simultaneously some young clergymen of the Church of England realized that the church must try to find a more moderate theology, one that would accommodate some of the Calvinists who had led the English Revolution and that would also speak to "men of business and dispatch," as one Cambridge clergyman put it. A similar desire to achieve compromise with the men of business was expressed by quite another group—the scientists, such as Robert Boyle, who were progressive in their social views yet supportive of the church and the monarchy. Their problem was that, heretofore, science often had been attacked by the church, not embraced by it. How, then, could one create a science that would sit well with an English elite who believed in God and king?

The new science of Copernicus had first flourished in Catholic, not Protestant, Europe. During the early seventeenth century, in Florence, Galileo proclaimed this science as a body of knowledge, independent of theology, that was interesting in itself and that promised to bring a new control over nature. In his published defense of the new science, *Dialogue Concerning the Two Chief World Systems* (1632), Galileo aggressively proclaimed it as a body of learning of particular relevance to laymen who had worldly interests. He said that the complexity of scientific learning and the potential power it conferred rendered science unfit for the common man (or for women in general); in effect he made a bold play for support from the Florentine aristocracy and merchants.

This proclamation of the relevance of science to the laity was perceived by powerful Florentine clergymen as a direct assault on their authority, and they took to their pulpits to denounce both this prophet of science and his message. They appealed to the Inquisition for assistance, and in the short run the Inquisition proved more powerful than Galileo and his allies. Yet the tension he gave voice to, between the old scholastic learning of the clergy and the universities and the new science of special

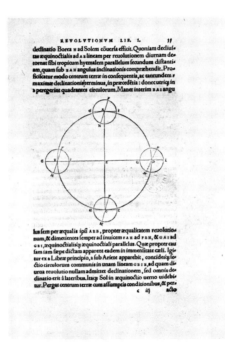

◄◄ Ottavio Leoni, **Galileo Galilei.** 1624. Engraving. *Ex. no. 81*

◄ Copernicus, **On the Revolutions of the Heavenly Bodies.** 1543. The first treatise to hypothesize that the earth revolved around the sun, in direct contradiction to the geocentric theory favored by the Catholic church, it was condemned and placed on the *Index* in 1616. *Ex. no. 56*

► Galileo, **Dialogo.** 1632. The Inquisition summoned Galileo to Rome to defend the *Dialogo*, which supported Copernicus. The book, in which characters representing conflicting astronomical schools discuss their views, was placed on the *Index. Ex. no. 55*

concern to lay elites, dominated the intellectual life of seventeenth-century Europe.

It is difficult to overestimate the importance educated people attached to Galileo's condemnation by the Roman Inquisition in 1633. At the time, much of Europe was at war over which religion would dominate the Holy Roman Empire. The power of Spain and its own Inquisition threatened to overwhelm the relative independence of the Protestant cities and principalities in Germany. The Dutch Republic feared for the survival of its newly won independence from Spain, and thinking people came to realize that new ideas of any sort were now seen to be threatening by both church and state.

In this atmosphere, the French scientist Descartes left Catholic Paris for the relative freedom of Leiden and its university in The Netherlands. Presses outside of the control of Spain or the Inquisition, eager to profit from the publicity of Galileo's condemnation, took up the publishing of science books with particular energy. They sold well. Descartes, in his *Discourse on Method* (1637), explained why that should be so. The foundation of scientific method lay in having the self-confidence to think one's own way to the laws of nature. The exploration of the universe began in the self ("I think, therefore I am") and ended, ultimately, with mastery over nature.

By 1665, and with the support of local magistrates eager for the new science, many Dutch universities openly taught Cartesian ideas as preferable to medieval scholasticism. The impetus for the acceptance of the new science came from a wealthy commercial elite that was independently Protestant and republican, as well as oligarchic. The opponents of Descartes—for instance, in The Netherlands during his lifetime—tended to be Calvinist clergy. They were allied with the people and with the universities against powerful magistrates, merchants, and landlords who wanted a philosophy of nature that expressed, as well as reinforced, their growing self-confidence. The anti-Cartesians, in Utrecht, for instance, attacked Descartes for his egoism and "vanity," and raised the specter of atheism. Many of his opponents were also followers of medieval scholasticism, and believed that Aristotle as modified in the fourteenth and fifteenth centuries offered an adequate explanation of physical reality.

Although the Dutch Republic in its *Gouden Eeuw* (Golden Century) became the publishing capital of Europe, the political, religious, and scientific consensus which lies at the heart of much of modern liberal thought came in the first instance from England. There, scientists such as Robert Boyle had supported a moderate revolution in the 1640s and then abandoned the revolution out of fear that the lower classes, led by Levellers and Diggers (such as Winstanley), would rebel. After the revolution the scientists wanted to establish the new science as an ally of the restored church and monarchy. To do that, however, required that the Anglican clergy respond to the new science in a very different spirit than had the priests of Galileo's Florence or the Calvinist ministers in Descartes' Utrecht.

What was needed was a science that supported a liberal and tolerant Christianity, one that would appeal to the laity and one that, when allied to the established church, might serve a strong but constitutionally bound monarchy. In the service of the state such a science would enhance the growth of empire and industry. The establishment of the Royal Society of London in 1662, by Boyle and his friends, with the assistance of a royal charter, laid the foundation of that alliance of state, science, church, and laity. The society received the right to publish science books under its own imprimatur—effectively giving its approval to some scientific ideas and not others—and it sought to form alliances with liberal clergymen, landed gentry, and leaders of the commercial sector.

The intellectual consensus that emerged had a profound impact on the nature and practice of censorship. The more radical uses to which the new science had been put, by Bruno, for example, or by freethinkers who argued that nature was a sufficient explanation upon which to base the laws of the new science, were now repudiated.

By the middle of the seventeenth century, as we have seen, there were many naturalists who had used the writings of Descartes, among others, to argue for a scientific naturalism as an alternative to Christianity. Indeed in Cambridge, in the 1660s, the science of Descartes was attacked by clergymen as a form of atheism. Yet these same clergy did not seek a return to scholasticism such as was the case in many continental universities of this period. Instead Anglican clergymen, impressed by how the new science of Boyle and the Royal Society could destroy scholastic assumptions about nature and hence undermine the teaching authority of the Catholic clergy, supported scientific investigations and publications and joined the Royal Society in large numbers. Gentlemen bought scientific books for themselves and their children, and believed that science and liberal Christianity would respect the power of the state, and hence their power as expressed by the will of the king in parliament.

Among the young students at Cambridge impressed by this consensus between science and liberal Protestantism was Isaac Newton, and on the basis of it he repudiated Cartesian science, which he too thought led to atheism. Without that repudiation Newton could not have formulated the law of universal gravitation that he finally published, under the auspices of the Royal Society, in the *Principia* of 1687. By the late seventeenth century, we find that the scientific ideas promulgated by the major scientists, Boyle and Newton, and their followers had been made to support liberal Protestantism. In other words, science and Protestantism in alliance were adopted by the ruling landed and commerical elites, who saw religious toleration—and hence a relaxation of censorship—as a way of consolidating state power in the service of wealth, commerce, and industry.

The alliance of scientists, liberal clergymen, and literate members of the elite who wished to retain their landed wealth while expanding their commerical activity, made possible a freer market in ideas. The market was one aspect of the deep political changes occurring late in the seventeenth century, which in 1688 produced the bloodless but successful Glorious Revolution. William, Prince of Orange and Stadholder of the Dutch Republic, was called upon to assume the English throne, but not until he and his wife Mary (daughter of James II) acknowledged parliament's independent right to govern. From that moment, parliament and king exercised joint political authority.

The landed and commercial elites, which had won this great victory over the throne and now controlled parliament, proceeded to take a decisive step in the history of censorship over ideas in print. Acting with the advice of philosopher John Locke, who had argued for religious toleration in his *Letter on Toleration*, published in The Netherlands in 1689, parliament allowed the Licensing Act to lapse in 1695. No longer did a publisher have to obtain a license from the local office of censorship (usually run by an ordained cleric) to publish a book.

In fact, after 1689 parliament preferred a relatively free press to accommodate the various political parties and factions that were vying for public support. Political pamphlets poured from the presses, and since neither of the dominant political parties—Whigs and Tories—held a clear monopoly over the electorate, censorship was minimal. The new atmosphere of freedom to publish had a spillover effect in all aspects of thought and communications. Men who called themselves freethinkers, or deists, or pantheists could publish with the same small presses that printed the weekly and even daily newspapers hawked about the streets and coffee houses in London and the provinces.

In the early eighteenth century, printing became a major business that benefited from the relative political stability of the nation. It was but one aspect of the commercial activity of the merchants and entrepreneurs whose growing importance from the mid-seventeenth century onward had helped to create the new alliance of scientists and clergymen. The growth of literacy, a process somewhat independent of the political upheavals that produced the consensus we have just described, also increased the marketplace for books and ideas.

By 1700 we can see the emergence of a new type of literary figure. These were men, and a few women such as Mary Astell, the first English feminist, who tried to live from the earnings of their pens. Some sold their talents to politicians or publishers; others were persons of considerable literary talent, like Alexander Pope and Jonathan Swift, who made good livings from their publications, even though they regarded the publishers who bought their books as thieves who paid as little as possible for their talent. A new literary world of reader, publisher, and writer had come into existence.

This world depended upon a relative freedom of the press, which itself was dependent upon a new intellectual consensus. It assumed that scientific ideas, and by extension intellectual pursuits, would entertain and divert practical men from religious wars or political rebellion. Provided government did not overtly interfere with their pursuits and interests, and preferably supported them, such men of business might be allowed "to read sullenly and silently" in their coffee houses or homes—to use the phrase of one suspicious clergyman—and even think heretical thoughts while getting on with what mattered: the enclosing of fields, the mining of coal, the selling of wares and the buying of labor, the patenting of new devices, the paying of taxes, and not least the buying of annuities out of which parliament and king might finance both foreign wars and the Bank of England. Among the most frequent users of this freer press were the clergy themselves, who took up their pens to exhort those who could afford their sermons and tracts. They urged them to be industrious in their callings, to bend their self-interest in the service of the public good, to support organized religion, and to turn their backs on heresy and irreligion. Not to be undone, the promoters of the new science, many of them clergymen themselves, also published a voluminous quantity of books for the laity that explained in simple mechanical terms the wonders of Newton's science.

Throughout much of the eighteenth century other educated Europeans, interested in science and material progress, and hostile to churches led independently of the state by rich and powerful clergy, looked across the Channel to England with envy. As compensation they seized upon English science, as well as upon English political writings, which the booksellers of London and The Hague were eager to supply them in a variety of European languages. By the 1730s every European city of any size had its literary societies, or scientific clubs, or masonic lodges where literate gentlemen might discuss the ideas they read in books supplied from all over Europe.

For governments still actively involved in the censorship of books, such groups presented problems. Who knew what kind of books aristocrats, gentlemen, or even shopkeepers might get their hands on and circulate among themselves? Indeed, one of the most fascinating historical puzzles to unravel is the circulation of clandestine literature throughout the eighteenth century. Copies of that treatise of the three impostors turn up nowadays in every major European library, demonstrating that their donors had once kept them in their homes or bookshops. The private letters of eighteenth-century publishers reveal a remarkable eagerness to supply customers with whatever they wanted: sermons, books on science,

NOVA ✠ REPERTA.

¹Americe. ²Lapis polaris. ³Ignibus
Amata puluis. ⁴Imprimi volumina.
⁵Rotisq; iugis indita hora ferreis.
⁶Hyacum. ⁷Ab igne stilla. ⁸Fila serica.
⁹Sißphæq; prisco operta cuncta sæculo.

ALOYSIO ALAMANNIO FLOR.ᴺᴼ
I. STRAD. INVENT. DD.

▲   Theodore Galle, **Title Page to** *New*
Inventions. Ca. 1600. Engraving. *Ex. no. 83*

▶   Johann Kepler, **The New Astronomy.**
1609. In this major treatise Kepler
demonstrated the elliptical orbits of the
planets around the sun, thus proving
Copernican theory. The book was placed on
the *Index* at about the same time that Galileo
was warned not to write or teach about the
Copernican theory of the universe. *Ex. no. 57*

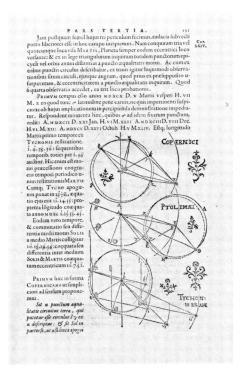

penny novels, hymnals, almanacs, literary masterpieces, pornographic stories, political tracts, or assaults on the king, aristocracy, or clergy.

The result of this traffic in books was a new culture, described at the time as "enlightened." Its assumptions about the value of learning and its dissemination rested upon a political, scientific, and religious consensus that had first been articulated in the aftermath of the English Revolution. The consensus had served the interests of a landed and commercial elite whose power had been rendered secure as a result of the revolution. The culture of the Enlightenment was, in the first instance, either indifferent to or hostile toward the needs and abilities of the people. During the eighteenth century, however, the boundaries of literacy increased and made access to the culture of those elites more and more commonplace. Under the impact of literacy and printing, ideas developed by elites to serve their interests soon acquired universal significance. The democratic tendencies within the republic of letters—the radical side of the European Enlightenment—eventually gained concrete political expression in the revolutions of the late eighteenth century, in the artisan movements to be found in the American colonies, The Netherlands, and Belgium, and, most important for European history, in France.

When the French revolutionaries used the writings of Locke or Milton, or when the democratic thinker Jean-Jacques Rousseau first formulated his ideas about popular sovereignty, they did so from French translations of works published in Holland and disseminated illegally by publishers in Switzerland or France. From the perspective of the absolute monarchs, it was always necessary to control the press; the problem was that by 1700 that meant controlling the whole of Western Europe.

SOURCES

The classic work on the history of the printing press is by Elizabeth Eisenstein, *The Printing Press as an Agent of Change* (Cambridge: Cambridge University Press, 1979). For the life of Giordano Bruno the best study is by Frances Yates, *Giordano Bruno and the Hermetic Tradition* (London: Routledge & Kegan Paul, 1964); Galileo's problems with the church are summarized in a new essay by Olaf Pederson, "Galileo and the Council of Trent: The Galileo Affair Revisited" (*Journal for the History of Astronomy*, vol. 14, 1983, pp. 1-29). The French system of censorship is ably described in Joseph Klaits, *Printed Propaganda under Louis XIV: Absolute Monarchy and Public Opinion* (Princeton: Princeton University Press, 1978). For the freethinking circles of Paris, see J.S. Spink, *French Free-Thought from Gassendi to Voltaire* (rpt. New York: Greenwood Press, 1969). There is no single book in English on the history of Dutch printing, but readers may consult Margaret C. Jacob, *The Radical Enlightenment: Pantheists, Freemasons and Republicans* (Boston: George Allen & Unwin, 1981). For the ferment of the English Revolution, consult Christopher Hill, *The World Turned Upside Down* (New York: Viking, 1972); and for the formation of the consensus after it, see James R. Jacob and Margaret C. Jacob, "The Anglican Origins of Modern Science: The Metaphysical Foundations of the Whig Constitution" (*Isis*, vol. 71, 1980, pp. 251-267). A basic introduction to the Enlightenment is provided by Roy Porter and Mikulas Teich, eds., *The Enlightenment in National Context* (Cambridge: Cambridge University Press, 1981).

5

The Eighteenth Century: Control and Revolution

EUGENE CHARLTON BLACK

In spite of a growing rhetoric of freedom, the eighteenth century remained an age of control. Hierarchy and unthinking obedience reached into every corner of the culture. Husbands regulated wives, fathers dominated families, elites ran institutions, and sovereigns ruled countries. Capacity and habit as well as regulation and authority modulated the conventions of behavior and discourse. As the century unfolded, the spread of prosperity and literacy, growing social mobility and urbanization, and the formulation of challenging theories about the nature of authority and the relationship between citizen and state eroded social and legal discipline and weakened the power of the state. The revolutionary surge at the end of the century saw France, England, and the infant United States frantically, almost hysterically, attempt to reestablish domestic discipline through legal controls of expression, in societies where conventional social controls had, or appeared to have, broken down.

Eighteenth-century society divided between those who could read and those who could not. Urban communities, embracing a significant and strategically placed fraction of the total population, had a considerably wider reading public than the formally literate. At pubs, cafes, coffee houses, inns, churches, and a wide variety of secular organizations, the literate read, selectively, to the illiterate, and the network of discourse reached outward from all of these to others with whom they, in turn, talked during the course of daily life. Public events demanded a ritual literature prepared well in advance. No execution, the greatest spectator sport of the eighteenth century, lacked its "Dying Speech and Confession of . . . " circulating through the alcoholic savagery of an enthusiastic public. So the ballad, the broadsheet, the print, the newspaper—even the book—reached well beyond the circles of the conventionally literate culture.

Where habits of mind control behavior, law and formal regulation are unnecessary. Social discipline suffices and legal discipline is redundant, even offensive. Those insensitive to community prejudice or careless of social authority will be jostled. The retainers of offended gentlemen cudgeled the young Voltaire. John Wilkes, not yet in command of the London mob, feared for his safety as much as a trial verdict and fled to Paris in 1764. Tar and feathers as well as cudgels threatened colonial American publishers when tempers flared during the Stamp Act crisis or in the passions of 1774–75. Should custom and convention falter, however, regulation and authority were never far away. Legal control—licensing, censorship, prosecution after publication—varied in rigor and extent over time and place. The abolition of licensing acts in England in 1695, for example, ended prior restraint upon publication, which had proven both ineffective and awkward. Parliament did not, however, intend to permit "license": the common law doctrine of seditious libel remained as a guardian against totally free expression in print. Seditious libel meant any "false, scandalous and malicious writing" that had "the intent to defame or to bring into contempt or disrepute." Once accused, pleading the truth of one's statement aggravated the offense: it was neither defense nor mitigation.

However fettered expression might be, the eighteenth century offered enormous opportunities. The educated and lettered aspired to that total command of knowledge that led Denis Diderot and his associates to assemble the *Encyclopedia.* To serve this new world thirsting for words, moreover, the "profession" of journalism came into being. Aspiring journalists, some brilliant, some hacks, swarmed to Paris and London in search of the rewards of Grub Street. Historian Robert Darnton has

EUGENE BLACK is Ottilie Springer Professor of Modern European History at Brandeis University. His books include *The Association: British Extraparliamentary Political Organization, 1769-1793* (Cambridge: Harvard University Press, 1963); *European Political History, 1815-1870: Aspects of Liberalism* (New York: Harper & Row, 1967); *British Politics in the Nineteenth Century* (New York: Harper & Row, 1969); *Victorian Culture and Society* (New York: Harper & Row, 1973). Among several major series of which he has been sole or co-general editor is the Harper & Row *Documentary History of Western Civilization,* 36 vols.

▶ Jean Huber, **Voltaire Portrait Studies.**
Ca. 1777. Etching. *Ex. no. 140*

▶ **Taking of the Bastille.** 1789. Engraving.
Ex. no. 127

tracked through this *demi-monde* to explain the tortuous routes to success and the twilight world of survival from which revolutionary and government spy or censor (often the same person) could rise.

Although at no time and in no country was there ever total freedom of publication and expression, the general eagerness for new information and literature formed a constant pressure in favor of greater access to printed works. This reached its logical conclusion early in the French Revolution, when royal authority collapsed and new restrictions had not been constructed or been deemed necessary. A hothouse growth spawned hundreds of newspapers and countless pamphlets, prints, and broadsheets. Earlier, the French book trade had itself undergone a transformation, between 1770 and 1778, and by the 1780s all of the important and many of the minor provincial centers had their own newspapers. Beneath the elite institutes and academies were various private literary societies, relatively easy of access, that extended the range of readers well beyond those who could actually afford to buy these hundreds of publications. As these developments slowly altered the habits of communication, the dominant groups in the population—the nobles, the bourgeoisie, even the shopkeepers and artisans—began to share a common set of ideas, words, and culture, expressed, as historian William Doyle has elegantly argued, in the *cahiers* (the grievances or instructions) of the nobility. The relative ease with which the revolutionaries enacted their program between 1789 and 1792 testifies to the success of the intellectual transformation, whatever constraints might have been imposed along the way.

Censorship in France before 1788 reveals some of the conflicts that shook not only France but England and her American colonies, as new habits of mind took shape and new ideas about authority were argued in print. During the late seventeenth century, Louis XIV and his ministers had no use for dissent, and employed censorship to curb criticism and controversy. Such commentary on public affairs as circulated went hand to hand by manuscript or was published abroad, usually in Holland.

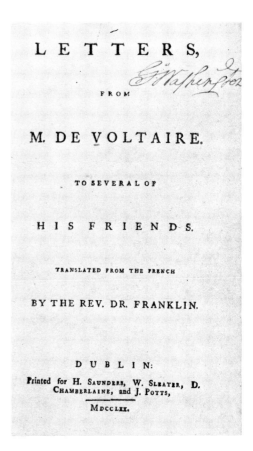

▲   Voltaire, **Letters . . . to Several of His Friends.** 1770. In the classical tradition of Cicero and Pliny, certain of Voltaire's letters were published in book form. Since the author was so popular among eighteenth-century readers, his works reached a wide audience; this is George Washington's copy. Although the letters were never censored, they discuss many censorship issues current at the time. *Ex. no. 99*

◄   **Révolutions de Paris.** 1789. This newspaper was one of many publications that sprouted in France after the collapse of effective censorship in 1788. *Ex. no. 129*

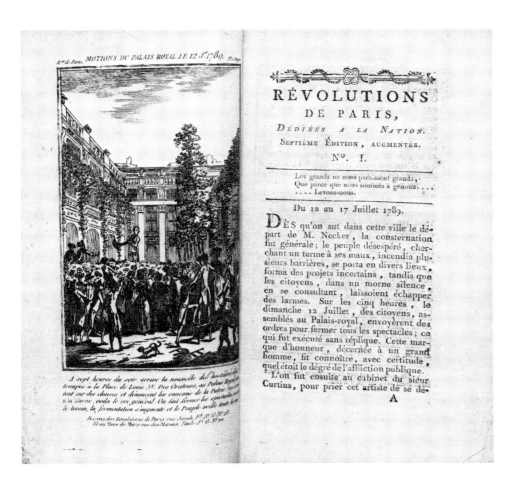

Nothing formally changed after the Sun King's death in 1715, but the Regency proved either less capable of or less interested in suppressing publications which would never have seen the light of day in the France of Louis XIV. Vigorous government censorship returned from 1723, although the floodgates, once opened, could never be entirely shut. Half-measures and compromises continued to erode control: many times publications were neither sanctioned nor banned, merely permitted to appear. Malesherbes, the great magistrate who managed government censorship from 1750 to 1763, understood that rigorous suppression could no longer work in a world which had an unappeasable appetite for new books. His answer was to control numbers, allowing rarity to ensure respect, and to attempt to confine knowledge to a sophisticated elite. Under his aegis, Diderot's *Encyclopedia* (1751–80) appeared, surviving unmolested until 1759 as it might not have done in France either before or after. To his friend Turgot, the reforming minister of Louis XVI, Malesherbes defended his strategy against a critic:

> But how can he say this periodical enjoys my patronage because I don't ban it? Can't he see that it's like holding the chief of police responsible for every case of pox contracted in the brothels because he tolerates them and reserves his police units for combating cutthroats?

To slow the import market, heavy tariffs were levied upon books published abroad, an extension of Malesherbes's tactics of controlling volume and raising price. Such moderation proved another casualty of French humiliation in the Seven Years' War (1756–63). Malesherbes, who had helped Rousseau publish *Emile* (1762), fell from favor and was dismissed from office in 1763.

Chancellor Maupeou reversed the relatively liberal policies of Malesherbes. Neither reinvigorated censorship nor Maupeou's attack on those obstructive bastions of aristocratic privilege, the law courts or *parlements*, could resurrect faltering absolutism. Maupeou went, and the *parlements* returned with the new king, Louis XVI, in 1774. A pleasant, simple, and pious man who would have made an excellent locksmith and clockmaker, Louis XVI was revolted by the license and irreligion of the Paris gutter press and insisted the police stop the traffic. It proved too late. The *parlements* occasionally prosecuted offensive works (as did the *parliaments* of Virginia and Massachusetts and Pennsylvania) and had them publicly burned. Such measures often served the function of "Banned in Boston" in the first half of the twentieth century: What better way to achieve advertisement and status in the Parisian salons than condemnation by stuffy provincials?

All authorities and every group, moreover, now sought to exploit and mobilize public opinion through the printed and spoken word. Louis XVI abandoned the government's effort to control the *parlements* in 1774 out of respect for opinion formed, in the first instance, by books and pamphlets. By so doing he hopelessly compromised any serious effort to reform France from above. As political ferment bubbled through the 1780s, authorities and their challengers used or evaded the networks of control.

Censorship collapsed with the crumbling of royal authority in the winter of 1787–88. The *Declaration of the Rights of Man and Citizen* (1789) conceded freedom of the press, a ratification of the actual state of affairs. An orgy of publication lasted until 1791. Every view had its outlet, and Charles Joseph Pancoucke demonstrated how to provide for them all.

▼ Abbe Raynal, **Histoire philosophique et politique** . . . 1773–74. *Ex. no. 120*

▶ James Gillray, **The Zenith of French Glory.** 1793. Colored etching. A satirical English comment on the excesses of the French Revolution. *Ex. no. 146*

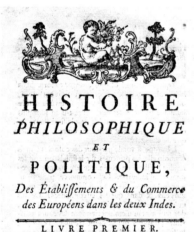

HISTOIRE
PHILOSOPHIQUE
ET
POLITIQUE,

Des Établiſſements & du Commerce des Européens dans les deux Indes.

LIVRE PREMIER.

L n'y a point eu d'événement auſſi intéreſſant pour l'eſpece humaine en général & pour les peuples de l'Europe en particulier, que la découverte du nouveau monde & le paſſage aux Indes par le cap de Bonne-Eſperance. Alors a commencé une révolution dans le commerce, dans la puiſ-fance des nations, dans les mœurs, l'induſtrie & le gouvernement de tous les peuples. C'eſt à ce moment que les hommes des contrées les plus éloignées ſe ſont devenus néceſſaires : les productions des climats placés ſous l'équateur ſe conſom-ment dans les climats voiſins du pole ; l'induſtrie

Tome I. A

The Zenith of French Glory; _ The Pinnacle of Liberty.

Religion, Justice, Loyalty & all the Bugbears of Unenlightend Minds, Farewell!

◀ After Swebach Desfontaines, **Assassination of Marat** (detail). From *Collection complète des tableaux historiques de la révolution française,* Vol. 2 (Paris: De L'Imprimerie Didot L'Aine, 1798), plate 83. *New York Public Library: Art, Prints and Photographs.*

Founder of the moderate but revolutionary *Moniteur* in 1789, which became the official paper in 1792 and survived as the instrument of every French government to the later 1860s, Pancoucke also published a newspaper for every faction. Most Parisian and French political activity came to center around clubs and a paper. None was more famous than *L'Ami du peuple,* published by Jean-Paul Marat, onetime physician to the king's brother, scientist at odds with the establishment, and an apprentice politician in the London of John Wilkes. Never at rest to the dramatic end of his peripatetic, tortured career in 1793, Marat brought street *patois* and slanderous invective to unparalleled refinement. His successor in style, Hébert with *Père Duchesne,* had to be silenced with the guillotine.

Books tumbled forth as well. Restif de la Bretonne, who had earlier skirted the gray area between sentimentality and pornography with *Le Paysan perverti* (1775), took advantage of the opening to begin publishing his monumental political, social, and moral critique *Monsieur Nicolas.* All authors and publishers, however, were "at risk." Displeased politicians, irritated factions, even an outraged populace might exact a fearful price for literary offense.

Since state and society could be damaged by words, the government determined to reimpose order through legal discipline. Censorship officially returned in 1791, although leakage remained considerable. The Constitution of that year guaranteed freedom from suppression prior to publication but substantially enacted the existing Anglo-American system; seditious libel or offenses against morality could be and were prosecuted. Authors and publishers confronted possible persecution for opinion. After the spasms of Jacobin Terror, the Directory manipulated opinion through bribery and coercion. French governments, like the Pitt administration in England and the Adams and Jefferson presidencies in America, managed public sentiment through an adroit mixture of subsidy and persecution.

Napoleonic France saw censorship reach bizarre lengths. By 1802, not merely newspapers, publications, and theatrical productions but even private correspondence came under the purview of authorities. From modest beginnings, lists of forbidden words expanded to include Bourbon, usurper, tyrant, sovereign people, social compact, as well as references to French defeats or unpleasant allusions to members of the Bonaparte family. Textual "corrections" of every play before performance converted tragedies into ludicrous comedies. At the same time, the idea of a free press marched through Europe with French arms and constitutions. The substance behind the form remained much the same as in France, varying slightly from region to region. Italy had relatively benign censorship, Bavaria severe, for no particular reasons beyond, perhaps, native taste and tolerance.

Across the English Channel, anxiety about the French Revolution precipitated a steady erosion of freedom of expression. The radicalization of the revolution, the execution of Louis XVI, and the opening of the Anglo-French war generated fear and played havoc with civil liberties. To conventional constraints, ranging from taxation of publications to prosecution or its threat under long-standing statutes and the common law, were added new measures of regulation and control. Conservatives imitated liberal social reformers in organizing pressure groups, but now the targets were those institutions providing for the "diffusion of knowledge." The authorities closed or brought under control reading rooms and circulating libraries; magistrates threatened public houses, coffee houses, and inns with loss of license should they take material of an "irreligious, immoral or seditious tendency."

▶ William Hogarth, **John Wilkes Esqr.** 1763. Engraving. *Ex. no. 141*

While the press remained surprisingly free in many respects, leading Wellington to complain that news stories were actually threatening his military operations in Spain, the "trade in sedition" came in for hard times. An unprecedented number of trials for seditious libel were brought before English juries. The law asked the jury to determine simply whether or not the accused had actually published the material in question. Fox's Libel Act of 1792 gave the jury the right to decide whether or not the material was libellous. Juries, however, were generally drawn from the ranks of the well-to-do and socially conservative. When public passions ran high, the jury-serving burghers and gentlemen of England were as likely as the most reactionary judge to stamp as seditious anything thought to bring king and constitution into "contempt or disrepute." John Thelwall, an actor, author, and reformer, once indicted for treason, later convicted of seditious libel, and much involved in radical agitation could find no London landlord in 1795 willing to rent him a small lecture hall. And this in spite of Thelwall's willingness to assume all legal risks.

Prosecutions on this scale were unprecedented earlier in eighteenth-century England. State action was unnecessary. Custom coupled with fear of offending authorities or community sensitivities effectively constrained expression. Political, religious, or moral critiques could be severely punished. Many were not. John Cleland was neither indicted nor punished for writing *Fanny Hill: Memoirs of a Woman of Pleasure*, although that book proved a moral and legal liability for the next two centuries. Cleland also enjoyed the patronage of the powerful Duke of Grafton, a leading politician in mid-eighteenth-century England.

Legal recourse was available and could be wheeled into action whenever authorities took serious offense. John Wilkes, a highly cultivated gentleman-journalist, *bon vivant*, and politican provided the excuse and occasion. Wilkes had squandered a fortune and seen his political friends removed from office. Cut off from political patronage, he turned to journalism, a new world of opportunity for London as it was for Paris. Jean-Paul Marat, recently come from France, learned his trade in the Wilkes school. In 1763 Wilkes published, in No. 45 of his paper *The North Briton*, an uninhibited attack on the king's ministers for their compromises in bringing an end to the Seven Years' War. Since Wilkes was a member of parliament and a gentleman, this might have passed as excessive but not actionable political discourse. Wilkes, however, called King George III a liar, and that was too much. When the government, spurred on by an irate sovereign, prosecuted Wilkes for seditious libel, he took up the challenge and turned the incident into a civil liberties case. An illegal search of Wilkes's premises also produced an *Essay on Woman*, a tedious but clearly obscene burlesque of Alexander Pope's famous *Essay on Man*. The double indictment, both political and moral, saw Wilkes expelled from the House of Commons in January 1764.

After a five-year exile in France, Wilkes returned to England in February 1768 to stand, first unsuccessfully for the City of London and then successfully for the county of Middlesex. Imprisoned twenty-two months for blasphemy and libel, repeatedly expelled from the House of Commons, Wilkes translated each reverse into a public triumph. Subscribers paid his £1,000 fine and enormous debts. Political partisans made him the dominant figure in the City of London and the metropolitan area. Returned again, in 1770, to a parliament which did not dare to throw him out, Wilkes fought and won yet another battle for freedom of expression. Using his elective office in the City of London and his position as member of parliament, he defied and overwhelmed the House of Commons in the Printers' Case of 1771, securing the right of the press to publish verbatim proceedings of parliament.

Although the hero of the London crowd, Wilkes had little respect for his adoring supporters. Yet whatever self-serving motives lay behind his actions, he had achieved significant gains for civil rights on the issue of general warrants (they became illegal), and for the rights of electors to choose their member, be he eligible to sit or not. He further secured the right to know by gaining full publication of parliamentary debates free from fear of prosecution for libel or violation of privilege.

Wilkes had felt the sting of punishment for both seditious libel and blasphemy, and had provoked a reaction unusual in its ferocity, probably because he had touched the person of the king. But Wilkes, although he never entirely abandoned his early radicalism, also came to speak for another England, a product of economic growth and urbanization, an England of new ideas as well as new opportunities. His politics were those of the merchants and tradesmen, the respectable masters and artisans who, by the last third of the eighteenth century, were coming to count for much in London. Wilkes, as they, had taken an uncompromising stand for law and order against mob rule in the destructive anti-Catholic Gordon Riots of June 1780. By the time of the French Revolution, however, the provocative issues of the day were no longer the issues of John Wilkes. The specter of political revolution and social upheaval in France inspired hopes for some but terror for more. Moderation, the middle ground in English political debate, evaporated before fear of revolution and the demands of what proved to be a quarter-century of war with France. Questions about American rights became, by translation, the issue of who and what were the commons of England. The deferential society that characterized the early part of the century began to fray and unravel.

The state had considerable resources to control opinion. The attorney general enjoyed special privileges when conducting libel cases, ostensibly because they might represent a clear and present danger to national security or morality. He could, in the first instance, try the crime before a special jury, one easily stacked with government employees and partisans. He could also file an *ex officio* information for libel. This enabled him to dispense with a grand jury finding. Far from hastening to trial, however, the *ex officio* information could be left dangling over the head of an author or publisher as outright intimidation. The filing itself put the individual at great expense (as much as £200) even if the case never came to trial. The costs of legal defense outstripped the resources of many authors and printers. The government took particular umbrage at the growth of inexpensive radical popular publications and responded with all its weapons. Royal proclamations encouraged conservative vigilantism; magistrates threatened to pull the licenses of pubs which continued to cater to radical political groups. The attorney general acknowledged in December 1792 that he held more than 200 *ex officio* informations in his files.

By far the most eloquent and most threatening statement of the radical position was Thomas Paine's *Rights of Man* (1791, 1792). Paine rejected all reformist arguments, openly embraced revolution, challenged every traditional institution, and propounded a new society as well as a new polity. Worst of all, in the eyes of authorities, the work was extraordinarily popular. The government struck hard. Paine made it easy for them by daring the secretary of state to indict him, then fleeing to revolutionary France. On December 18, 1792, a special jury convicted Paine of publishing a seditious libel. The conviction, a foregone conclusion, came in spite of the extraordinary forensics of Thomas Erskine, the greatest trial lawyer of his day and self-appointed spokesman of a modest civil rights movement. Much given to high drama, Erskine punctuated his four-hour closing summary speech by fainting once for the jury. That speech stands as a classic statement for freedom of the press, and it served to keep Paine's work alive. Once Paine had been convicted, every bookseller carrying the *Rights of Man* lay liable to prosecution, and anyone citing Paine's book was guilty by extension. Erskine's *Defence of Paine,* being a trial proceedings, was not actionable.

Prosecutions for seditious libel and *ex officio* informations proved so successful that in 1794 the government brought treason charges against the leaders of the principal radical reform organizations. Given the temper of the times, each individual could have been convicted of sedition, but Erskine and London juries prevailed against the excessive charge of treason. The noose on expression, nevertheless, drew steadily tighter. An Act of 1798 made the proprietor of a newspaper liable for whatever appeared on its pages. Even the newsboy, who might well be illiterate, could be imprisoned for selling a newspaper that the courts subsequently found seditious.

Such constraints were generally popular. Even those who teetered on the issue of political debate had no tolerance when the issue was blasphemy or irreligion. Thomas Erskine, that champion of freedom of expression, personally prosecuted Paine in 1797 for his broadbased attack on the Bible and Christianity in the *Age of Reason* (1794, 1795). Paine's proposition that "religion is a private affair between every man and his Maker . . . in which no third party has any right to interfere" ran afoul of the most deeply held values of the politically conscious public. Even when prosecutions against political writings declined in the second quarter of the nineteenth century, blasphemy and atheism roused the public and authorities.

Some last desperate writhings of the political reform movements in 1799 produced a trivial revolutionary conspiracy, and the government responded by imposing a system of registration on printers (which hinted at "prior restraint") and banning "Jacobinical" societies. They were charged with circulating "irreligious, treasonable and seditious" publications among the "lower classes of the community, either gratis or at very low prices, and with an activity and profusion beyond all former example." These powers remained in place through the Napoleonic era and into the early 1820s, tortured years of rapid economic growth, social stress, badly managed military demobilization, and considerable political turmoil. The pillory and public whipping returned briefly to vogue in a campaign to restore discipline in society by stamping out a flood of blasphemous and seditious publications. The punishment of the pillory for libel vanished again in 1816, another ill-considered and readily discarded wartime measure. Stamp duties, those contrived taxes on knowledge, were hammered down from 1825 to 1836, to disappear entirely in 1855. The attorney general's abused privileges in libel prosecutions were limited in 1819. Such excesses seemed almost embarrassing to "freeborn Englishmen."

No legislation could control the amusingly licentious and clearly seditious spate of publications surrounding the divorce trial of Queen Caroline in 1820. The case, which proved a matter of acute royal embarrassment and humiliation, firmly established the precedent of divorce-case reportage as the socially acceptable vehicle for salacious titillation. Lord Sidmouth, a cabinet minister much given to hysteria in such matters, even forbade his daughters to read *The Times.* After 1822, prosecutions for seditious libel were considered impolitic. Lord Campbell's Libel Act of 1843 finally tidied matters up, establishing essentially the definitions and procedure that obtain to the present. Social discipline, that hallmark of Victorian culture, would do the rest. The majesty of the law was rarely needed.

Americans shared the pattern of their British overlords with some exaggerations. Colonial societies were so many petty orthodoxies, punishing dissent or misbehavior with communal intimidation and legal assault. The foremost authority on the subject finds not more than half a dozen trials for seditious libel in colonial America, one of which, the Zenger Case in 1735, has gained much importance in history books while having had little impact on actual freedom of expression. Judges were probably far more tolerant of opinion than legislative assemblies, governors, and colonial councils. Political criticism would bring its author swiftly before the bar of a house unrelenting in its prerogatives, quick to punish, and intolerant of abuse. Political dissent went unpunished only when public opinion lay strongly on its side.

Newspapers, which came slowly to North America, tended originally to develop as adjuncts of the postal system, with postmasters editing the first successful sheets. Like booksellers and printers in general, local

▼   James Gillray, **Tom Paine's Nightly Pest.** 1792. Etching. This print comments on the problems besetting Paine after he was charged with seditious libel for publishing *The Rights of Man. Ex. no. 148*

TOM PAINE'S Nightly Pest.

newspaper publishers depended upon local support and patronage and were unlikely to ruffle community prejudices. But some individuals set caution adrift in the breeze. James Franklin, half-brother of Benjamin, enlivened Boston from 1721 to 1726 with his controversial and rather clever *New England Courant.* The suggestion that provincial officials might be overly sympathetic to the feelings of pirates brought him before those authorities and into prison, leaving young Benjamin to learn the trade by continuing the paper. James and his son soon sought the safer climate of Rhode Island, and Ben Franklin vanished to Philadelphia to produce the most successful newspaper of all, his *Pennsylvania Gazette.*

New York, not London, proved to be the setting for the first great seditious libel trial of the eighteenth century. John Peter Zenger thrived on controversy and loved politics. Exploiting the unpopularity of the gover-

◀ **Massachusetts Spy.** May 3, 1775. Newspaper. This is the first issue of the *Spy* printed in Worcester, after its publisher, the patriot Isaiah Thomas, closed his shop and smuggled his press out of Boston, away from British efforts to control reports about the growing unrest in Massachusetts. *Ex. no. 116*

nor, he vented his personal spleen on the hapless William Cosby. The governor and his colleagues responded through the courts. Zenger, arrested in November 1734, continued to edit his paper from prison for the next nine months. His spectacular trial occupies a place of honor in all histories of civil liberty. Andrew Hamilton, imported from Philadelphia to speak lines James Alexander (the true moving spirit in the whole business) had written for him, argued that the jury had the right to decide whether Zenger's articles were in fact seditious libels, not merely whether Zenger did or did not publish them. Alexander and Hamilton won acquittal for Zenger, something Erskine could not do for Paine. Zenger's triumph made him the hero of the New York streets in the same way that conviction made John Wilkes Lord Mayor of London.

The Zenger case, however, had much less influence on the law than on people like "Father of Candor" who speculated on the true meaning of liberty of expression. Neither in New York nor in other colonies were American publishers free from official censorship under breach of privilege or the laws of libel. The histrionics of the Zenger case were real, the findings intellectually marketable, and the case did ultimately become a precedent to which appeal would be made in both Britain and America. Free speech and a free press in America came to mean the right of angry merchants, bully boys, and professionals to damn British misrule, first in the Stamp Act Crisis and then in the cauldron of prerevolutionary agitation. But then as always, community prejudice and vigilantism controlled, they did not liberate, opinion.

The Zenger defense presumed that truth could not be a libel. The law, however, held that the truth aggravated a seditious libel. "Father of Candor" reminded an unheeding public and legal profession that this must never be so. Only a willfully false and malicious publication should be actionable, and only a jury should determine that fact. Yet, even the strongest libertarians conceded that the state might be criminally assaulted by words. After the Revolution, Americans had settled the issue of home rule and could address the issue of who should rule at home. In 1798 Congress passed the Alien and Sedition Acts, which were intended to silence Republican opposition to Federalist anti-French foreign policy. President John Adams, like his counterpart William Pitt in England,

Complaint from a Committee of Correspondence. July 29, 1773. During the period of the American War of Independence, patriots in many communities established committees of correspondence, which helped organize revolutionary activity and establish a framework for collective action by the colonies against England. The committees also functioned to suppress dissent. *Ex. no. 112*

thought of himself as introducing measures which, even if politically motivated and juridically abused, seemed legitimate responses to the threat of revolutionary ideas and the prospect of war with revolutionary France. The old formulas were still there: "any false, scandalous, and malicious writing" against the United States "with the intent to defame... or to bring... into contempt or disrepute...." Federalists attempted to clarify an ambiguous situation; that they also attempted to use it for narrow political advantage was in keeping with the politics of the day in Britain or France. The First Amendment of the Constitution enacted "no prior restraint" on expression, and Federalist clarification meant merely that otherwise the English common law should hold. The Sedition Acts, moreover, like Fox's Libel Act of 1792, allowed the jury to decide whether the matter was libellous or not. The American law, in fact, was far ahead of the British: the truth was supposed to be a defense, which it would not be in Britain until 1843.

Much is made of a "tyrant" Adams and a "libertarian" Jefferson, but each, in fact, used the courts to prosecute irksome publishers. Adams preferred federal courts; Jefferson those of friendly states. Both were attempting, unsuccessfully as things turned out, to bring order to the extremes of a hyperbolic political life that more than one historian has described as ordeal by slander. Neither Adams nor Jefferson nor any sitting justice of the day thought the First Amendment emancipated the seditious, the blasphemous, or the obscene. That it came to do so over the next century and a half, and that the United States became the ultimate haven for refugees persecuted for their words, has much to do with the nineteenth and twentieth centuries but little to do with the eighteenth.

The world was more similar than different in eighteenth-century France, Britain, and America. Governments might talk of "freedom" but believed in control. So, too, did the societies of which they were ultimately expressions. Only as social organization and the nature of the culture itself began to change did the substance of law and authority also change. Freedom came to mean undreamt-of things. We have all become the beneficiaries, as Leonard Levy put it, of a First Amendment "boldly stated if narrowly understood."

SOURCES

In general, see Robert Darnton et al., *The Expanding World.* Publications of the Society for Eighteenth-Century Studies (Philadelphia: University of Pennsylvania Press, 1979). For France, see Daniel Mornet, *The Intellectual Origins of the French Revolution* (New York: 1954; translated from the French edition of 1933); Robert Darnton, *Mesmerism and the End of Enlightenment in France* (Cambridge: Harvard University Press, 1968); *The Great Cat Massacre* (New York: Basic Books, 1984); and his excellent articles: "Reading, Writing, and Publishing in 18th-Century France" (*Daedalus,* vol. 100, 1971, pp. 232-237); "In Search of Enlightenment: Recent Attempts to Create a Social History of Ideas" (*Journal of Modern History,* vol. 43, 1971, pp. 125-127); "The Grub Street Style of Revolution: J.P. Brissot, Police Spy "(*Journal of Modern History,* vol. 40, 1968, pp. 301-327); and "The High Enlightenment and the Low-Life of Literature in Pre-Revolutionary France" (*Past & Present,* vol. 51, 1971, pp. 81-115). Also useful is William Doyle, *Origins of the French Revolution* (Oxford: Oxford University Press,

1980). For the Anglo-Americans, the best single account is Leonard W. Levy, *Legacy of Suppression: Freedom of Speech and Press in Early American History* (Cambridge: Harvard University Press, 1960), which in spite of the title covers both sides of the Atlantic. In addition, for Britain, consult Caroline Robbins, *The Eighteenth-Century Commonwealthman* (Cambridge: Harvard University Press, 1959); Arthur Aspinall, *Politics and the Press c. 1780-1850* (London: Home & Van Thal, 1949); Albert Goodwin, *The Friends of Liberty: The English Democratic Movement in the Age of the French Revolution* (Cambridge: Harvard University Press, 1979); Robert K. Webb, *The British Working-Class Reader 1790-1840* (London: George Allen & Unwin, 1955); and for the United States (in addition to Levy): James M. Smith, *Freedom's Fetters: The Alien and Sedition Laws and American Civil Liberties* (Ithaca: Cornell University Press, 1956), and Vincent Buranelli, ed., *The Trial of Peter Zenger* (New York: New York University Press, 1957).

▲ Edouard Manet, **Polichinelle.** 1874.
Lithograph. The authorities censored this print
because the face of the clown was thought to
resemble the president of France. *Ex. no. 199*

▶ Jean-Ignace Isidor Gérard, called
Grandville, and Eugène Forest, **Résurrection de
la censure.** 1832. Lithograph. This print
comments on the renewal of official
censorship by King Louis-Philippe. *Ex. no. 156*

It is generally held that the image is more powerful than the word, and this may be easily explained. For a student of semiotics it is the image, rather than the word, that most closely approaches what is being represented, appropriating some of its visual aspect, intermingling with it and, in a manner of speaking, even physically touching it. For the teacher the image is dangerous because of its immediacy, because it stands as both evidence and artifact, and because, through its ability to make its point without using words, it offers itself freely to whoever may be interested, while disguising its creator. For the politician the image is ruthless because it offers no opportunity for response: like an attack or a blow it interrupts and ends all discussion and permits no reply. Hence every image of a figure becomes an idol, every representation an illusion, every caricature a slander.

Before examining specific instances where the image has been censored, it is important to understand that the image is censored at least in part as a result of the efforts of a certain class of educated people—the guardians of knowledge—politicians, and *moralistes* who regard it only as a deceptive and empty imitation of truth. Empty because it represents mere physical reality without analysis or commentary; deceptive because it does represent physical reality, and for this sort of person true essence cannot be expressed through that kind of representation. The battle between image and word has raged for a long time, often influencing other controversies. On certain issues it continues today, more in Europe than in the United States; for example, in the condemnation of television or of the *bande dessinée* [a book of cartoon-strips on topics of broad general interest] as methods of learning. In French schools even the blackboard was long viewed with suspicion. Educational censorship of the image can be seen, for instance, in an anecdote related by the writer Anatole France, who like many *petit bourgeois* boys of his day learned Greek from a very dull grammar book, whose title can be translated as *The Garden of Greek Roots*. The book's frontispiece was a drawing of a young man dressed in

6

The Image in France

MICHEL MELOT

MICHEL MELOT, formerly conservator of the Department of Prints and Photography of the Bibliothèque Nationale (1967–1983) and its director (1981–1983), is currently director of the Bibliothèque Publique d'Information du Centre Georges Pompidou. He has written numerous works on prints, especially on the caricature: *L'Oeil qui rit: le pouvoir comique des images* (Fribourg: Office du Livre, 1974); *Dubout* (Paris: Trinckvel, 1979); *La Belle époque et son envers: quand la caricature écrit l'histoire* (Paris: Sauret, 1980); in collaboration with Anthony Griffiths and Richard S. Field, *L'Estampe: histoire d'un art* (Geneva: Skira, 1982; also available in English); and, forthcoming in 1984, *L'Illustration, des hiéroglyphes à la bande dessinée* (Geneva: Skira).

Translation by CATHERINE BROOKS.

the ancient Greek manner and opening the gate of a garden. This sober illustration, the only one in the book, appeared quite frivolous to the teacher, who tore it out before distributing the books to his students. Anatole France concluded that the teacher belonged to the generation which "taught dunces by telling them what to think."

Yet, at just this time, it was becoming difficult to teach students as if they were dunces, since modern life was coming to be based on knowledge derived from an empirical understanding of nature and the world of objects. Philosophers like John Locke in England or, much later, Jean-Jacques Rousseau in France had advocated images as models of knowledge connected intimately to "experience" and to the concrete; that is, related to the language of the senses and of nature, but also related directly to crafts and industrial production. When the general spread of images became inevitable at the end of the eighteenth century, images began to be used in an aggressive and militant way against the very class [the bourgeoisie] which had repressed them, which had sensed in them a threat against language and against the elite use of language of which that class was the master. This is why the caricature, whose highest moment came between 1750 and 1850, was not only an act of political subversion which attacked the questionable behavior and traits of politicians, it was also an aesthetic subversion, distorting that academic norm of representation which had been established as the accepted discourse. From this arose the second form of censorship against the image, the political.

Here the censor's interference was neither rare nor new. As early as 1694 two men were executed in Paris for having published an engraving that showed the French king entwined with four women who had been his mistresses. Even during the Revolution, when many restrictions on expression were lifted, the Paris Commune ruled against the vogue for caricatures that had grown up in imitation of English practice. On July 31, 1789 a decree was passed that allowed the publication of prints. Liberty was never total at this time, and on April 27, 1799 Bonaparte forbade

▼ Charles Philipon, **Project for a Pear Monument.** 1832. Lithograph. King Louis-Philippe's pear-shaped head is the basis for this satire on his anti-republican policies. *Ex. no. 157*

"merchants of prints from showing anything contrary to good morals or against the principles of government."

During the nineteenth century, censorship played a central role in French history. Not only was freedom of the press advocated as a major demand of the bourgeoisie against Charles X and his reactionary government, but it was the typographers, a trained and organized group directly concerned with the economic advancement of printing, who were the first to take to the streets in the rebellions of 1830. Charles's successor, Louis-Philippe, was supposed to grant full freedom of the press—in fact it was

◄   August Desperet with Jean-Ignace Isidor Gérard, called Grandville, **O July Sun, Come Quickly!** 1835. Lithograph. *Ex. no. 158*

◄   Honoré Daumier, **Liberty of the Press. Don't Meddle with It!!** 1834. Lithograph. *Ex. no. 189*

Ah! tu veux te frotter à la presse !!

L. de Becquet, rue Furstemberg 6.   *chez Aubert, galerie vero dodat.*

84

the precondition of his accession to the throne—as soon as he was installed, and he did. Two years later, in a judgment rendered on February 23, 1832, he sent Daumier and his editor, Charles Philipon, to prison for "exciting hatred and . . . injury to the person of the King." In the years following 1835 Louis-Philippe reestablished censorship of images and prints.

How can we explain this about-face? We are forced to the conclusion that a caricature cannot be evaluated in the same way as a text. A caricature, through its direct attack on the person's physical embodiment, works violence of the sort that is felt as a kind of physical assault. According to this very philosophical line of argument, pamphleteers, on the other hand, were allowed freedom of expression because they fought not with images but with words, noble weapons of the kind employed by the class of people who were accustomed to dueling with speech. Caricaturists fought with images, illicit arms, which struck without allowing any opportunity for defense or response, and which reached both specific targets and the larger public. What the law did not explain, however, is why only the Republican caricatures, especially those published in the paper *Charivari*, attracted a crowd every afternoon at the window of the printer Aubert, in the Passage Vera Dodat. And the art historians who reject the idea that an aesthetic quality can be born from a social movement have also been unable to explain this.

Behind educational and political censorship there stands a third kind, which claims a religious or metaphysical justification. It is necessary to reexamine the long history of the proscription of images by established religions—Jewish, Muslim, and, in certain areas and at certain times, Christian. But this must not lead us too far astray, for each situation has its particular characteristics. A common motif recurs in these religious proscriptions: the fear of the representation of the human figure, to the extent that one believes the figure is a divine form, and the concern that to reproduce it is to substitute it for God, to "believe in another God," as the

◀◀ Honoré Daumier, **Ah! You Want to Step on the Press!!** 1833. Lithograph. *Ex. no. 188*

◀ Honoré Daumier, **Lower the Curtain, the Farce Is Played.** 1834. Lithograph. *Ex. no. 190*

Second Commandment forbids, and thus to commit a sacrilegious act. This particular kind of censorship did not disappear completely with the conclusion of the iconoclast controversy [which raged in the Byzantine Empire during the eighth and ninth centuries, and saw the destruction of many religious images—icons]. All forms of religion teach a respect for the image: the image that pertains to the sacred, and especially the human image and the image of God. We find a striking example of this from the mid-nineteenth century, during the "liberal" phase (1865–1870) of the Second Empire, under Napolean III, when caricatures were again permitted, but only with the assent of the person caricatured, the victim of the caricaturist's pen. Out of this grew the bizarre fashion for the "great heads." André Gill, for example, was able to draw all of the celebrities of the day for one of his magazines without fear that this newly popular genre would encounter political repercussions. Alexander Dumas, approached to sit for a head, replied humorously that he would gladly permit someone to do a caricature of him since this would be the only portait that could possibly do him justice. The poet Lamartine, on the other hand, was furious at the request and refused publication of his face in a caricature, on the grounds that it would be, in his words, an injury to both God and to human nature. And so the taboos were not really overcome: the ancient human fear of standing before the distorted mirror, the menace latent in all perceptions, the refusal to manipulate the image as one would any other human creation or contrivance, the condemnation of the power of the image to make humankind into a monster as well as a god—this ancient mythic dread we behold, to our surprise, in the poet himself, a creator, but also a good man, a political man, as protective of his image as of his most cherished possessions.

All French revolutions have come into being under the call of freedom of the press. The history of censorship in the nineteenth century exactly follows the rhythm of the great moments of the nation's history. Freedom, suppressed in 1835, was reestablished in 1848 during the brief period of

▶ Goya, **Nothing. The Event Will Tell.** 1810-20 (published 1863). Etching. Part of a series, *The Disasters of War*, this etching was censored for its portrayal of the Napoleonic war in Spain. *Ex. no. 202*

▶ Edouard Manet, **The Execution of the Emperor Maximilian.** 1867. Lithograph. Archduke Maximilian of Austria went to Mexico, at the behest of Napoleon III, to establish himself as emperor. Mexican revolutionaries shot the archduke, ending Napoleon's American adventure. *Ex. no. 198*

▶▶ Goya, **They Make Use of Them.** 1810-20 (published 1863). Etching. From *The Disasters of War. Ex. no. 201*

▲   Félicien Rops, **The Abduction.** Ca. 1886.
Heliogravure. *Ex. no. 237*

the Second Republic, and was again suppressed by Napoleon III upon his *coup d'état* in 1852. Napoleon III fell on September 4, 1870; steps to free the press began on the fifth. In 1871, following defeat in the Franco-Prussian War, the new National Assembly chose to maintain censorship. As in 1830, it was repression of the press that incited the rebellion of March 18, 1871. This was a time when the Right, anticipating another restoration of the monarchy, was busy undermining the fragile foundations of a republic that was still seeking its own voice. The Republic was not established securely until January 5, 1879, the day the republicans gained a majority in the Senate, which had traditionally been conservative. On July 29, 1881 a law was passed that was to become very famous, one that replaced the old, complex, and repressive statutes regulating the press with an extremely liberal framework for governing press freedom. This law reflected the regime's commitment to democratic legislation based upon the right of expression.

The forms of censorship that we have enumerated are, it seems, extremely diverse in origin: educational, political, religious, and aesthetic. They have not disappeared today, but only occasionally do they lead to formal legal action, and even more rarely do they result in repressive legal judgments. There remains the most complex form of censorship—moral—and in particular, legislation against pornography. The law of 1881 abolished the concept of an "offense against opinion," but it retained two repressive provisions. The first was against anarchism, in response to a series of assassinations, begun in 1877, that were traumatizing European public opinion. The second, against obscenity, was partly in response to the then current fashion for publications designed to provide light entertainment to a public of newly affluent bourgeois. This was the era of Grevin and Willette drawings that often showed flimsily dressed women posed in vaguely obscene or risqué ways. This was also the era of *japonisme*, in which an elegant and erotic fashion attempted to avoid censorship through exoticism. There were several famous court cases at this time, against the satanic illustrations of Félicien Rops and, in 1887, the sentencing of Louis Legrand for an illustration, published in *Le Courrier Français*, entitled "Prostitution." This illustration would appear quite innocent today, and the French law, which still makes it possible to impose a two-year sentence on anyone who makes and distributes images that are contrary to good morals, has not been able to halt the invasion of Paris by "sex shops," which have already taken over Amsterdam and New York.

Meanwhile, with increasing frequency, modest eyes must look away from "indecent" advertising billboards. The battle against the offensive images has been taken up aggressively by the feminist movement, and in 1983 the French Minister for the Rights of Women began a campaign for passage of an anti-sexist law. One of the law's provisions would make it possible to censor all images presented solely "for the purpose of the sex of the person" (*en raison du sexe de la personne représentée*). Clearly this relates to women, but male homosexuals have also wanted to use it for their own protection. The law specifically applies to any representation that is stereotypical, demeaning, or degrading.

The opposing sides in this controversy each present strong arguments. The feminists want to prevent the image from being used to promote the cultural ideology of male domination over woman's body. Against the proposed law, on the other hand, accusations have been hurled of censorship, moral regimentation, and prudery. We note that the Ayatollah Khomeini, when he reimposed the wearing of the chador on women, proffered this same argument about protecting women, and who can say what image is "debasing" to women: erotic sex-object, or perfect secretary, or housewife, or stewardess? The debate was so lively in the French press during the spring of 1983 that the Minister of the Rights of Women had to promise to modify her text before proposing the new law to the National Assembly.

Behind the actual debate, it seems to me, it is not so much the status of women that is in question but that of the image. As this debate demonstrates, even in our own day, the reform of a doubtless contemptible reality requires yet another suppression of the image. The proposed attack on the image is exactly like that of the medieval iconoclasts against images and representations, as if in some completely magical way the figure itself could become a living part of the reality. Again we are burning an effigy. Rather than persist in believing that the image is reality, perhaps we would accomplish more by trying to understand that the reality of the image *is not* the reality to which the image refers; that the relationship is not simply a mechanical one and that, for this reason, the image manipulates qualities such as derision, aggression, and provocation in ways that are precisely *not* part of reality. But to undertake this analysis would be much more painful and difficult than to continue foolishly to believe, even today, that the image of a dog bites.

SOURCES

There is no recent general study on the censorship of images, but a number of works about the nineteenth century, the illustrated press, and Daumier have begun to open up this new area of investigation. In particular we should cite the work of Philippe Roberts-Jones, whose thesis on the illustrated press during the second half of the nineteenth century has unfortunately not been published in full, but which has nevertheless led to several publications: *La Presse satyrique illustrée entre 1860 et 1890* (Paris: Institut Français de Presse, 1956); *De Daumier à Lautrec* (Paris: Les Beaux-Arts, 1960), and *Le Caricature du Second Empire à la Belle Epoque* (Paris: Club Français du Livre, 1963). The same author has summarized the various laws on the press in an excellent article, "La Liberté de la caricature en France au XIXe siècle" (*Synthèses*, no. 165, 1960).

Books dealing with Daumier and with the origins of the illustrated press contain long passages on censorship. On Daumier the most recent bibliography has been published in a special issue of *Nouvelles de l'estampe* (no. 46/47, July-October, 1979) devoted to Daumier on the centennial of his death; and for the illustrated press in Europe in general there is material in the proceedings of the conference "Daumier et le dessin de presse" given by the Association Histoire et Critique des Arts, at the Maison de la Culture de Grenoble, in July 1979 (these proceedings constitute no. 13/14, first fascicle, 1980, of *Histoire et critique des arts*). For the twentieth century one should consult general histories of the press, for example, Alain Manevy, *Histoire de la presse 1914–1939* (Paris: Correa, 1945), or *Histoire générale de la presse française*, vol. 3, published under the direction of Claude Bellanger and Jacques Godechot (Paris: Presses Universitaires de France, 1972).

Social Purity and Freedom of Expression

JOEL H. WIENER

"Sedition, blasphemy, scurrility, and immorality, if they have not been quite kept out of newspapers, have dwindled down and have lost all their force now that enlightened public opinion has substituted a new censorship for that of the old benighted tyranny." If Henry Fox Bourne's observation, penned in 1887, is open to question, it is nonetheless broadly true. The period from the late eighteenth century to the early twentieth century marks a decisive transition in the history of censorship. It witnessed the effective ending of political control over the printed word in the West, a situation characterized by Alexis de Tocqueville as "a necessary consequence of the sovereignty of the people" and, similarly, by John Stuart Mill as "the necessity to the mental well-being of mankind (on which all their other well-being depends)."

As Western countries experienced the dissolution of monarchical and authoritarian rule, so too did press controls wane: initially in the area of politics, then, somewhat more slowly, where matters of religion were concerned. But as the "benighted tyranny" of political and religious censorship gave way to greater individual freedom, sexual and moral concerns became predominant in many areas of public and private life, and these altered the quality of press freedom. Only in the twentieth century have such moral restraints substantially diminished.

The decline of censorship was spasmodic rather than smoothly continuous. There was not, as has frequently been assumed, a direct progression from restraint to freedom. Some forms of public restraint on the printed word disappeared slowly; others ceased to be used regularly. Until the middle decades of the nineteenth century, vestiges of official censorship continued to be part of the fabric of public life in France, Britain, and even the United States. During these years literacy became widespread and there emerged an enlarged market for printed works. At the same time the new technology of steam accelerated the productivity of print and diminished its cost.

Yet to a degree, governments in the West continued to try to maintain control over printed works. In France, where during much of the century the political life of the nation was affected by a series of revolutions, strict censorship or prior restraint of printed materials existed fitfully and inefficiently under the supervision of police and local prefects until 1881. In Britain, prior censorship of publications had ended in 1695 with the lapsing of the Licensing Act of 1662, which had established an official system of licensing books and newspapers. No attempt was made to reestablish it. In the United States, the First Amendment to the Constitution stipulated that Congress "shall make no law ... abridging the freedom of speech; or of the press." As interpreted by the courts, this effectively did away with remnants of prior censorship existing from the colonial period.

But in all three countries some controls on the printed word remained in force until the middle of the century or later, and these constituted a post facto form of censorship. Britain's system of press regulation was much more complex and burdensome than that of the United States. There were taxes on newspapers, periodicals, and advertisements; statutory provisions for the registration of printers; a requirement that securities be posted with the government against successful libel prosecutions; and local ordinances that provided for the licensing of vendors. All of these devices were used to hamper freedom of the press. For example, the "taxes on knowledge" (affecting newspapers, paper, and advertisements) were introduced in 1712 primarily as a means of checking the growth of periodicals. Subsequently they were used to drive cheap radical

JOEL H. WIENER has written widely on Victorian life and culture and on British foreign and domestic policy. In addition to numerous articles and reviews, he has authored *The War of the Unstamped* (Ithaca: Cornell University Press, 1969); *Radicalism and Freethought in Nineteenth-Century Britain: The Life of Richard Carlile* (Westport, Connecticut: Greenwood Press, 1983); and the forthcoming *Innovators and Preachers: The Role of the Editor in Victorian Britain* (Westport, Connecticut: Greenwood Press). He currently chairs the Department of History at City College, City University of New York.

publications from the field and were not fully repealed until 1861. No comparable controls existed in the United States after colonial times, when a Massachusetts tax on newspapers and advertisements had been used to curb press freedom. But there were informal restraints on the press, such as the granting of state and local contracts to favored printers and a tight supervision of the mails and ports of entry to assure that certain controversial works did not circulate freely. In France, "caution money" as a security against prosecution was required up to 1870, and taxes on the press were in effect throughout most of the century.

In all three countries statute or common law provisions (or a combination of both) established a framework of restraint based upon seditious and blasphemous libel. This was intended to make it difficult for critics of the government and of religion to operate with impunity. In the late eighteenth and early nineteenth centuries, prosecutions for sedition and blasphemy occurred in all three countries, particularly as the fear of revolution and of political unrest increased. Several hundred radical publishers and printers in Britain were prosecuted for sedition between 1792 and 1848. Sympathetic juries acquitted many of them. But some well-known writers and publishers, including William Cobbett, Leigh Hunt, Henry Hetherington, and William Lovett, as well as distributors of books and newspapers, were sentenced to terms of imprisonment and fined for seeking to give practical expression to their belief in a free press. Some of the more controversial political writings of Thomas Paine were effectively proscribed in Britain after their publishers were convicted of sedition.

In the United States, editors and publishers were much less likely to be prosecuted, owing principally to the lack of a perceived revolutionary threat from abroad. Yet in the early nineteenth century, Federalists and Republicans brought charges of sedition against opposing newspaper editors under the Sedition Act (1798–1801) and, more questionably, under federal and state laws defining public libel. In France, where printed materials could be banned before publication, sedition and blasphemy were less central to the government's strategy. But here too, editors and publishers risked occasional prosecutions for libel and lengthy terms of imprisonment and heavy fines.

If political apprehensions loomed large during the first half of the nineteenth century, a time of growing reform movements and the organization of extralegal pressure groups, so too did concern over the well-being of established religion. Except in France during the Restoration (1814–30), churches could no longer impose direct legal restraints on the press. But religion was still uniformly regarded as the mainstay of morality and stability. Without protection for religion, and particularly Christian scripture, it was believed that nothing was defensible. Even more than with political criticism, governments of the early nineteenth century (backed by clergymen) moved against "blasphemers, atheists, and deists": in short, against all those who sought to "defame and revile" religion and to diminish the ability of the "lower and illiterate" classes to "bear up against the pressure of misery and misfortune." For a time the deist writings of Paine and Elihu Palmer were proscribed in Britain, and during the 1820s and 1830s the atheist publisher Richard Carlile was imprisoned for almost ten years as a result of his attempts to circulate such writings. During the early part of the century, French critics of religion faced the possibility of a death sentence for blasphemy and Britons might be transported to Botany Bay after a second offense. Deists and atheists in the United States, though likely to be treated more leniently, also ran the risk of heavy fines and imprisonment.

The infliction of harsh punishments for political and religious libels and, in Britain and France, the enforcement of complementary restraints on the press, represented an effort by government to keep the press under some form of official control. It was intended primarily to meet the challenge to the existing system from political democracy (in Britain and the United States) with its secularist connotations, and from the threatening image of the urban mob. In Britain, the perception of this threat was greatest between 1792 and 1819 and, briefly, in the early 1840s, and this led to increased attempts at repression.

A struggle on behalf of a free press took place throughout much of the West during this period, with publishers making effective use of their best weapon—publicity. When the political threat waned (in the United States with the coming of the Jacksonian "age of reform" in the 1830s, in Britain with the decline of the Chartist movement in the late 1840s), prosecutions for political and religious sedition became largely a thing of the past. After a period of comparative liberalism in France, controls on the press were tightened once more between 1852 and 1870 by the Emperor Louis Napoleon. But these were shortlived, and by the second half of the century, the words of James Grant, a British journalist, seemed almost everywhere to be coming true: that print was destined "to become the great ruling power, not in this country only, but throughout the whole area of civilization." Little remained of earlier official forms of censorship other than occasional prosecutions for sedition or blasphemy.

However, the achievement of formal press freedom, though energetically fought in political terms, was perhaps the easier part of the task. For to some extent it was inevitably tied to the evolution of democracy. As individual freedom increased, and the right to vote became widespread, so too did freedom of print. Furthermore, technology was for once on the side of liberty. At a time when books and newspapers were proliferating, and a mass readership was coming into existence, overt forms of political and religious censorship no longer seemed viable. How could external controls, whether before or subsequent to the act of publication, be applied effectively when circulation was in the hundreds of thousands? Targets could not be easily identified; and when attempts were made to isolate such targets, legal action was likely to fail because of the size of the audience and the strength of the opposition. For better or worse, it seemed preferable to allow political and religious structures to work out their development without interference. Thus, excepting isolated cases which have recurred periodically up to the present time, formal censorship has largely disappeared along with the political and religious conditions that, seemingly, brought it into existence.

But as formal control lapsed by the middle of the nineteenth century, a "new censorship" of restraint and inhibition began to take its place. This was a more subtle form of censorship because it mirrored the complexities of the new world of print. Governments were involved only to a marginal extent, as they occasionally sought to suppress an "obscene" publication or to bring an errant author to judgment for corrupting the morals of the community. Much more frequently did they rely on others to do the job for them: publishers and editors of magazines, newsagents, librarians, readers and, perhaps most effective, the prospective offenders themselves. In short, governments called on public opinion to purify printed matter. For with the decline of political radicalism and the elaboration of a more unified popular culture, a public consensus was coming into being which shunned immorality and all forms of sexual indecency. It was largely influenced by middle-class values and the claims of respectability. Some

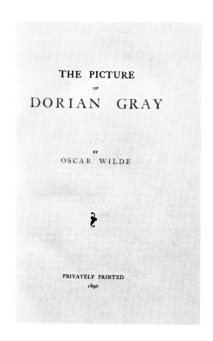

writers resisted its pressures, like the novelist George Moore or, more poignantly, Oscar Wilde who, in the Preface to *The Picture of Dorian Gray,* declared: "There is no such thing as a moral or an immoral book. Books are well or badly written. That is all." But the message of this public opinion was the same almost everywhere: eliminate touches of indelicacy and, above all, be sure that language and style are fit for family reading.

The "Victorian" decades were not rigidly puritanical, it has often been noted, and concealed many unconventional thoughts and acts beneath their tranquil cover. But the pressure to conform to an external ideal dominated, and not until well into the twentieth century did this repressive moral outlook cease to operate effectively. Only then could authors of a wide range of printed materials express themselves freely about matters of personal morality.

The origins and form of Victorian censoriousness continue to elicit debate. It has been shown, for example, that a similar urge to censor existed to some extent during the eighteenth century. Much has also been made of the importance of evangelical and humanitarian impulses that rose to prominence by the early nineteenth century. Religion, in its battle with secularism and materialism, took up whatever weapons lay at hand. But the religious impulse gradually declined, and religious groups exercised a diminishing hold on public opinion. When we look into the reasons for the appearance of the new censorship, therefore, we must turn to a more encompassing explanation.

Not religion, so much, but the effects of industrialization and urbanization helped engender new impulses to limit freedom of expression in print. These two forces, which ran with increasing speed and force throughout the nineteenth century, created vast new pools of wealth and dramatically altered the demography of Europe and North America. Growing wealth and opportunities for upward mobility offered the possibility of true social respectability to millions of people who, in the old agricultural and rural economy, would have been relegated to the unedu-

▲   Oscar Wilde, **Picture of Dorian Gray.**
1890. *New York Public Library: Berg Collection.*

▶   Robert Dale Owen, **Moral Physiology.**
1835. An early treatise on birth control, Owen's book circulated freely for many years. The passage of stricter anti-obscenity laws in England in 1857 and the Comstock Laws in the United States made its publication illegal. *Ex. no. 211*

cated urban poor or to the impoverished "idiocy of the countryside" (to use the words of a contemporary social commentator, Karl Marx). But respectability carried its own burden of values, among them the shutting out of what was not respectable, and this lay at one root of the urge to censor.

At the other root lay a deeply ambivalent attitude toward the city. As society became increasingly urban, it seemed to many observers that the new environment was destroying the old values, the old religion, and old respect for order and authority. The message seemed clear, whether spoken in Manchester, Lyons, or on the Lower East Side of Manhattan: keep the crowd at bay if society is to avoid anarchy. Yet, the city also provided a field for the expression of the new wealth and respectability that became increasingly evident as the nineteenth century unfolded. City life encouraged people to define a new status for themselves, and offered possibilities for achieving and exhibiting prominence and importance. Once gotten, however, these cherished possessions needed protection from the many forces that worked against social harmony and public order; women and children were perceived as especially vulnerable to these corrosive influ-

◀ François Lucas, after Etienne Jeaurat, **Example to Mothers.** Ca. 1762? Engraving. *New York Public Library: Art, Prints and Photographs, Cadwalader Fund.*

L'EXEMPLE DES MERES.
Tiré du Cabinet de Monsieur Damery,
Chevalier de l'Ordre Royal Militaire de St. Louis.

ences. Eventually, perhaps, all of society could be transformed into respectability.

By the mid-nineteenth century, a system of moral self-censorship existed in many parts of Britain, the United States, and France. Thomas Bowdler's *Family Shakspeare*, published in London in 1818 but even more widely circulated in the United States, is the best example of this. Bowdler's purpose, explicitly stated, was to excise whatever "cannot with propriety be read aloud in a family" or "is unfit to be read aloud by a gentleman to a company of ladies." The result was a Shakespeare without badinage, shorn of sexual passages from *Othello, Henry V,* and other plays, and with entire sections of text excised. Collections of the writings of Gibbon, Smollett, Oliver Goldsmith, and others were similarly "bowdlerized" by aspiring editors. Novelists toned down their own books. Dickens repudiated anything that "might be impurely suggestive to inferior minds (of which there must necessarily be many among a large mass of readers)"; while Thackeray likewise extolled an age in which writers "no longer have the temptation to write so as to call blushes on women's cheeks." George Eliot, whose private life lay well outside the domain of Victorian

▶ After Arthur Boyd Houghton, **My Treasure.** 1861. Wood engraving. *Ex. no. 193*

▼ William Makepeace Thackeray, **Vanity Fair.** 1848. In his contrast between Amelia Sedley and Becky Sharp, Thackeray plays upon many of the cultural themes that seem so typically Victorian today. Amelia is the nineteenth-century ideal of the proper young Englishwoman—modest, self-effacing, and chaste. Becky, born of a French mother and an artist father, lacks the moral rigor of Amelia; her loose ways and vanity are, to Thackeray, the antithesis of feminine propriety. *Ex. no. 177*

respectability, did little to ruffle the feathers of her readers. When informed by her publisher that a line in *The Mill on the Floss* was too strong, she obligingly changed the description of Mrs. Moss from a "patient, loosely-hung, child-producing woman" to a "patient, prolific, loving-hearted woman."

Editors and publishers frequently censored the work of their contributors. Henry Alford, the editor of the *Contemporary Review*, refused to publish an article by Edward Dowden until the word "nude" was changed to "unclothed." Thackeray, during a stint as editor of the *Cornhill Magazine*, would not publish in their original language some of the writings of Anthony Trollope and Elizabeth Barrett Browning. For example, he rejected the Browning poem *Lord Walter's Wife* because "our readers would make an outcry" over its "account of unlawful passion felt by a man for a woman." He also terminated the publication of John Ruskin's tract of social criticism, *Unto This Last*, when some readers began to protest against its controversial tone. In the United States, Stephen Crane's novel *Maggie: A Girl of the Streets* was issued in a small pseudonymous edition because of its delicate subject matter. When Appleton's, a commercial

▼ **The Family Shakspeare,** edited by Thomas Bowdler. 1818. The popularity of this expurgated edition of Shakespeare produced a new word in the English-speaking world: bowdlerize, first used in 1838. *Ex. no. 173*

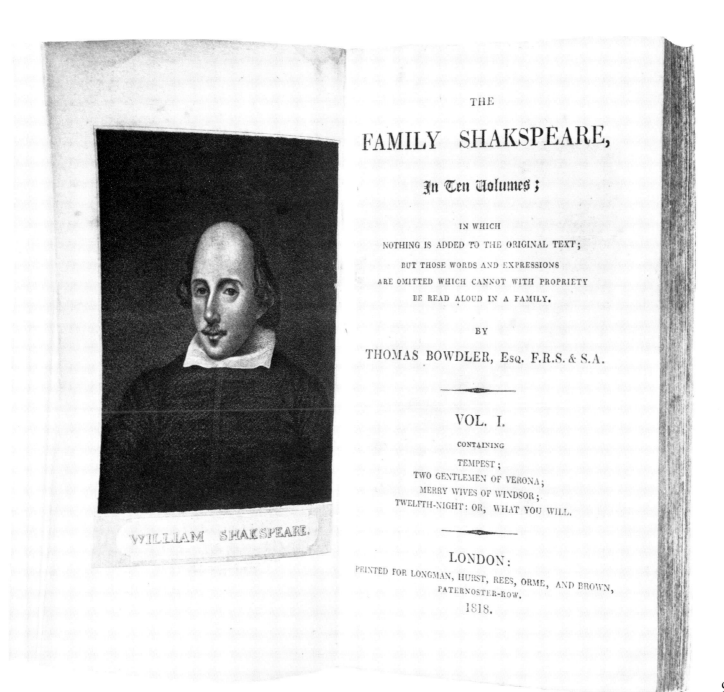

THE

FAMILY SHAKSPEARE,

In Ten Volumes;

IN WHICH

NOTHING IS ADDED TO THE ORIGINAL TEXT;

BUT THOSE WORDS AND EXPRESSIONS
ARE OMITTED WHICH CANNOT WITH PROPRIETY
BE READ ALOUD IN A FAMILY.

BY

THOMAS BOWDLER, Esq. F.R.S. & S.A.

VOL. I.

CONTAINING

TEMPEST;
TWO GENTLEMEN OF VERONA;
MERRY WIVES OF WINDSOR;
TWELFTH-NIGHT: OR, WHAT YOU WILL.

LONDON:
PRINTED FOR LONGMAN, HURST, REES, ORME, AND BROWN,
PATERNOSTER-ROW.
1818.

WILLIAM SHAKSPEARE.

publisher, finally agreed to publish the novel in 1896, it did so on condition that Crane tone it down. He consented reluctantly and told his editor: "I have carefully plugged at the words which hurt. The book wears quite a new aspect . . . ."

Most authors went along with the system but a few fought tenaciously for freedom of expression, at least insofar as their own books were concerned. Thomas Hardy occasionally acted as self-censor, as when he bowdlerized *Jude the Obscure* for *Harper's Magazine*; according to the editor of *Harper's*, the "purism" of the American magazine's readers was "undoubtedly more rigid here than in England." But at other times Hardy deftly circumvented the censoring proclivities of those he dealt with. For example, when *Far From the Madding Crowd* appeared in the *Cornhill Magazine*, it did so without any reference to Fanny Robin's illegitimate baby. Yet this omission was subsequently clarified and the cuts restored when Hardy published the novel in book form. Gustave Flaubert initially accepted minor excisions in the serial publication of *Madame Bovary*. After more cuts were requested, however, he told Laurent Pichat, a coeditor of *La Revue de Paris*: "*Well I'll do nothing more*, not a correction, not a deletion, not a comma less, nothing, nothing. . . . One can't whiten negroes, and one can't change the blood of a book, one can only impoverish it, that is all." Similarly, George Moore fought hard against the "censorship" of Mudie's Circulating Library and of W. H. Smith and Son, the wholesale newsagent and book dealer. He refused any of the cuts demanded by these "mere tradesmen." As a result, Smith would not stock his 1883 novel, *A Modern Cover*.

Ultimately, the sanction of the law might be used against those authors, publishers, and editors who refused to give ground in the area of personal morality. Formal controls had been largely discarded insofar as politics and religion were concerned, but this was not the case for "obscenity." Until well into the twentieth century, censorship received public support when its objective was the elimination of smut and pornog-

▶ After George Du Maurier, **Distressing Dilemma for Our Young Bachelor Surgeon!** 1865. Wood engraving. *Ex. no. 196*

DISTRESSING DILEMMA FOR OUR YOUNG BACHELOR SURGEON!

raphy. Magistrates and juries had a high rate of conviction, particularly where commercial pornographers like William Dugdale or the Frenchman Poulet-Malassis were involved, rather than well-known literary figures. France saw about 55 obscenity cases a year between 1876 and 1906, most of them ending in conviction. In the United States, obscene libel was recognized as an offense in common law, and a number of books and newspapers were prosecuted during the decades before the Civil War. Throughout the nineteenth century, British magistrates regularly impounded pornographic tracts and pamphlets and issued orders for their destruction.

Nineteenth-century obscenity laws, made use of only when more subtle means of censorship failed, were problematical, however, if only because there was no satisfactory definition of obscenity. In Britain and the United States, the legal definition of obscenity until the 1930s was that of Lord Cockburn in the Hicklin Case (1868): printed materials are obscene if they have a tendency "to deprave or corrupt those whose minds are open to such immoral influences." Similarly, in France, where the law against obscene publications was strengthened in 1881 at the very time that other restrictions on the press were being removed, obscenity was an offense against "public and religious morality and good taste." The test of immorality was not the undermining of an objective credo, but whether or not the susceptibilities of individuals had been offended, however much these might vary. In Britain a respected commercial publisher like Henry Vizetelly could be imprisoned in 1889 for publishing excerpts from Emile Zola's novels *Nana* and *La Terre*; the studies of Havelock Ellis on homosexuality were barred for more than ten years under threat of a prosecution for obscenity. In France, sections of Charles-Pierre Baudelaire's collection of poems, *Les Fleurs du Mal*, were proscribed and Flaubert was prosecuted unsuccessfully for *Madame Bovary* (though without his costs being paid). Walt Whitman's *Leaves of Grass* was banned by the city of Boston in 1882 after a local publisher was threatened with prosecution. Similarly contro-

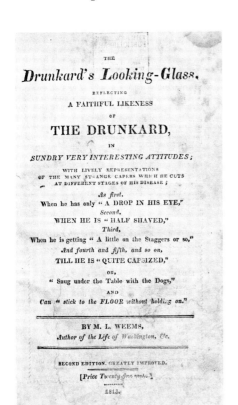

EMBARRASSING.

Nervous Spinster (to weary Old Bachelor). "OH, MR. MARIGOLD, I'M S⟨
FRIGHTENED! MAY I TAKE HOLD OF YOUR HAND WHILE WE'RE GOIN⟨
THROUGH THIS TUNNEL?"

◀◀ Parson Weems, **The Drunkard's Looking-Glass.** 1813. Washington's biographer also wrote moralistic exhortations to virtue. *Ex. no. 171*

◀ After Charles Samuel Keene, **Embarrassing.** 1869. Wood engraving. Victorian ideals of domestic life helped shape attitudes about what was permissible to write. *Ex. no. 194*

versial were the actions taken against publishers of birth-control pamphlets, who were routinely prosecuted for circulating "obscene" material.

The activities of private pressure groups added a further complication to obscenity prosecutions. Such groups had been active in the history of moral censorship ever since the appearance of the Society for the Suppression of Vice in Britain in 1802. They proliferated in post-Civil War America. Their goals included the elimination of all forms of immorality: gambling, drink, desecration of the Sabbath, swearing and, above all, the dissemination of obscene and pornographic works, however loosely defined. Many obscenity prosecutions were initiated by private associations (some by means of entrapment); while, simultaneously, organizations like the New England Watch and Ward Society and the New York Society for the Supression of Vice, both founded in 1873, pressured publishers, editors, and newsagents into withdrawing support from controversial writers. The Obscene Publications Act of 1857, which consolidated the British laws on obscenity, was passed in response to private pressure.

In the United States, numerous state laws, town ordinances, and federal regulations regarding obscenity, including tighter controls on the movement of printed works through the Post Office and their importation from abroad, were likewise a response to the actions of private societies. Undoubtedly, the most important product of private initiative was the Comstock Act of 1873, which consolidated various statutes and regulations dealing with "obscene, lewd, and lascivious" publications; in section 211 it specifically barred birth-control materials from the mail. Anthony

▶ **Abstract of the Proceedings of the Society for the Suppression of Vice.** 1803. The Society was organized in London to combat immoral, obscene, or blasphemous conduct and publications. This is one of its earliest pamphlets. *Ex. no. 170*

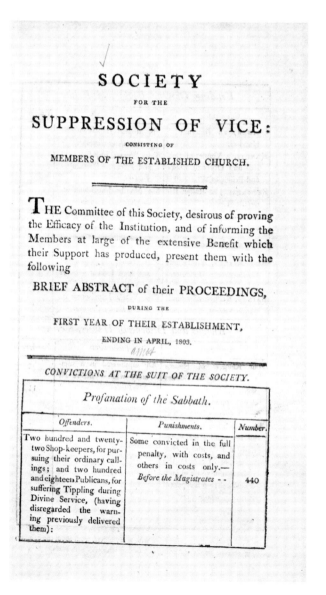

SOCIETY

FOR THE

SUPPRESSION OF VICE:

CONSISTING OF

MEMBERS OF THE ESTABLISHED CHURCH.

THE Committee of this Society, desirous of proving the Efficacy of the Institution, and of informing the Members at large of the extensive Benefit which their Support has produced, present them with the following

BRIEF ABSTRACT of their PROCEEDINGS,

DURING THE

FIRST YEAR OF THEIR ESTABLISHMENT,

ENDING IN APRIL, 1803.

CONVICTIONS AT THE SUIT OF THE SOCIETY.

Profanation of the Sabbath.

Offenders.	Punishments.	Number.
Two hundred and twenty-two Shop-keepers, for pursuing their ordinary callings; and two hundred and eighteen Publicans, for suffering Tippling during Divine Service, (having disregarded the warning previously delivered them):	Some convicted in the full penalty, with costs, and others in costs only.— *Before the Magistrates - -*	440

Comstock, a religious fanatic whose motto was "Morals, Not Art or Literature," was the secretary of the New York Society for the Suppression of Vice. Acting in the belief that "if you open the door to anything, the filth will all pour in and the degradation of youth will follow," he worked to enact not only the 1873 statute but also a series of state and local laws. These laid the basis for the prosecutions of leading birth-control advocates such as Edward Bliss Foote and Margaret Sanger; the exclusion of works by Rabelais, Boccaccio, Voltaire, and other "obscene" writers; the destruction of many obscure books and illustrations and the prosecutions of newsagents and bookdealers who sold them; and successful legal actions against several significant literary works including Elinor Glyn's *Three Weeks* (1908) and Theodore Dreiser's *The Genius* (1916). "Comstockery" (as dubbed by George Bernard Shaw) gave its name to a genera-

◀ Theodore Dreiser, **Sister Carrie.** 1900. Doubleday printed Dreiser's first novel, but had second thoughts about its strong realism and decided not to distribute it. *Ex. no. 204*

tion of puritans but it was, in truth, the culmination of the "new censorship," both self-imposed and externally applied.

The nineteenth century was, then, a significant era in the history of censorship. Formal censorship largely died out and freedom of print in a political and religious framework flourished. The words of John Milton in the *Areopagitica* may appropriately be applied to this period: "That which purifies us is trial, and trial is by what is contrary." But the new morality of sexual restraint was a formidable opponent. For even as sexual mores began to change, many people clung tenaciously to the old repressions, and these affected the output of books and newspapers even until today. If Victorian prudishness is a thing of the past, its inhibiting tendencies remain with us still.

SOURCES

There is no general history of censorship adequate for the nineteenth century as a whole. The best study of literary censorship, limited in its coverage to Britain, is Donald Thomas, *A Long Time Burning: The History of Literary Censorship in England* (London: Routledge & Kegan Paul, 1969). Alec Craig, *The Banned Books of England and Other Countries: A Study of the Conception of Literary Obscenity* (London: George Allen & Unwin, 1962) is similar in scope but much less scholarly. Lucy Maynard Salmon, *The Newspaper and Authority* (London: Oxford University Press, 1923) has a broad focus, though concerned primarily with military censorship. Norman St.John-Stevas, *Obscenity and the Law* (London: Secker & Warburg, 1956), provides a fine study of British obscenity laws. Theodore Zeldin, *France, 1848-1945*, vol. 1, *Ambition, Love and Politics* (Oxford: Clarendon Press, 1973), has material on the obscenity laws in France, and Enid Starkie, *Flaubert: The Making of the Master* (New York: Atheneum, 1967), contains a useful chapter on the prosecution of Flaubert for the publication of *Madame Bovary*.

On newspaper censorship, both H. R. Fox Bourne, *English Newspapers: Chapters in the History of Journalism*, 2 vols. (London: Chatto and Windus, 1887), and Frank Luther Mott, *American Newspapers: A History of Newspapers in the United States Through 260 Years, 1690 to 1950* (New York: Macmillan, 1950), contain useful information. Irene Collins, *The Government and the Newspaper Press in France, 1814-1881* (London: Oxford University Press, 1959), is an account of political press censorship in France during the nineteenth century. John Lofton, *The Press as Guardian of the First Amendment* (Columbia, South Carolina: University of South Carolina Press, 1980), provides a detailed history of press reaction to censorship in America. William H. Wickwar,

The Struggle for the Freedom of the Press, 1819-1832 (London: George Allen & Unwin, 1928), is an excellent study of the struggle against the press laws in early nineteenth-century Britain. Joel H. Wiener, *The War of the Unstamped: The Movement to Repeal the British Newspaper Tax, 1830-1836* (Ithaca, New York: Cornell University Press, 1969), is a detailed history of the repeal of the British "taxes on knowledge."

On moral censorship, Paul S. Boyer, *Purity in Print: The Vice-Society Movement and Book Censorship in America* (New York: Charles Scribner's Sons, 1968), offers a dispassionate analysis which concentrates on the 1920s. David J. Pivar, *Purity Crusade, Sexual Morality and Social Control, 1868-1920* (Westport, Connecticut: Greenwood Press, 1973), has interesting material on the activities of censoring groups in late nineteenth-century America. Oscar Maurer, " 'My Squeamish Public': Some Problems of Victorian Magazine Publishers and Editors," *Studies in Bibliography*, vol. 12 (1959), pp. 21-40, is an important article that deals with Victorian publishers, editors, and the "new censorship." Paul S. Boyer, *Urban Masses and Moral Order in America, 1820-1920* (Cambridge, Massachusetts: Harvard University Press, 1978), contains a fine analysis of the cultural and intellectual reasons for moral repression in America, while Maurice J. Quinlan, *Victorian Prelude: A History of English Manners, 1700-1830* (New York: Columbia University Press, 1946), is incisive on the revolution in moral attitudes in Britain. Peter Fryer, *The Birth Controllers* (London: Secker & Warburg, 1965), and Linda Gordon, *Woman's Body, Woman's Right: A Social History of Birth Control in America* (Harmondsworth, Middlesex: Penguin Books, 1977), provide information about attempts to censor birth control publications.

When Thomas Jefferson insisted that among "certain unalienable rights" are "Life, Liberty, and the pursuit of Happiness," his words reflected an eighteenth-century theory which held that it is human nature to strive for freedom, love, justice, truth, and individuality. From the end of the American Revolution to the beginning of World War I, except for a brief period during and following the Civil War, most white male citizens pursued their "unalienable rights" without serious government interference. Since World War I, the opportunity to exercise such rights has been extended to many previously excluded groups. The assimilationist vision of a "melting pot" society has given way to the ideal of pluralistic democracy, which encourages diverse groups and interests to compete, without having to surrender their distinctive identities, for a share of the American Dream. Ironically, while we have come closer than ever to achieving equality of rights among our citizens, we have also begun to encounter new threats to the integrity and value of our rights. One threat has been the development, in the United States and other postindustrial nations, of technologies that provide means by which government bureaucracies exercise growing control over the freedoms and rights of citizens. Yet, in the final analysis, the willingness to use technology for this end reflects the readiness of the citizenry itself to accept a diminution of its freedoms and rights, in the name of a greater good or in the fear of a greater evil. For much of this century, especially during the past few decades, the perceived good and the perceived evil have often turned on the tensions generated by a growing diversity in American society.

A technologically enhanced bureaucracy is capable of exerting enormous control over private actions and public information. In a free society such control, in the form of restrictions on rights protecting individual actions or on information contained in books, magazines, television, and movies, is commonly defined as censorship. When censorship is systematized, it is called surveillance. The effectiveness of this kind of comprehensive censorship is gauged by how much intelligence information can

◀ **Letter of Appeal from member of the Executive Committee of League for National Unity.** March 9, 1918. The league was organized to mobilize public opinion to support the war effort. This letter was an election appeal urging League members to defeat anyone opposed to the war. *New York Public Library: Rare Books and Manuscripts.*

JOAN HOFF-WILSON, Executive Secretary of the Organization of American Historians and Professor of American History at Indiana University, is a specialist in twentieth-century foreign policy and politics. Her numerous publications include *Herbert Hoover: Forgotten Progressive* (Boston: Little, Brown and Co., 1975) and *Balancing the Scales: Changing Legal Status of American Women from the Colonial Period to the Present* (Bloomington, Indiana: Indiana University Press, forthcoming). She is currently working on a study of the Nixon presidency.

8

The Pluralistic Society

JOAN HOFF-WILSON

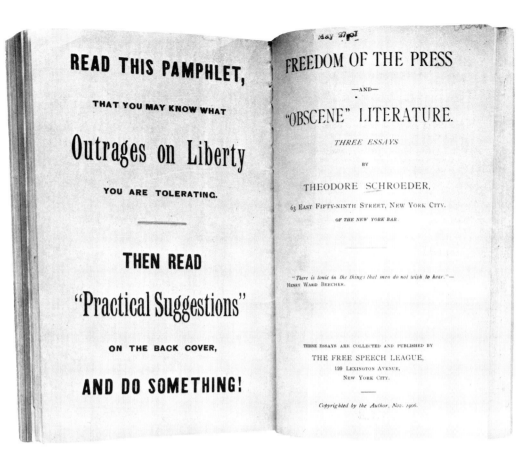

▶ Theodore Schroeder, **Freedom of the Press and "Obscene" Literature.** Ca. 1906. Schroeder was a well-known lawyer who argued for greater freedom of expression and against obscenity laws. *Ex. no. 208*

▶ **Scopes Trial.** In 1925, teacher John T. Scopes was tried for violating the Tennessee state law that prohibited teaching Darwin's theory of evolution. Scopes was convicted in one of the most famous courtroom confrontations in American history. Here, the court is listening to defense attorney Clarence Darrow (not shown) apologizing for some remarks he had made. *Ex. no. 259*

be gathered about targeted groups or individuals and by how much "sensitive" government information can be protected. "The extreme form of censorship" in the modern world may not, therefore, be "assassination" as George Bernard Shaw claimed in 1921, but rather an obsession with collective secrecy and management of information on the part of the state, which, in turn, requires encroachments upon the individual's right to keep secrets and engage in a wide variety of private acts. In the twentieth century surveillance of this type has been practiced by governments spanning the entire political spectrum, proving that Big Brother can function behind many ideological masks.

Most Americans are aware only of the less systematic form of censorship, the one which involves control over print or media material. They are less likely to be concerned about technologically sophisticated forms of censorship, which threaten their civil rights or civil liberties. Civil rights are those specific First Amendment guarantees of freedom of speech, press, and religion which have been expanded and incorporated into the Fourteenth Amendment through judicial interpretation. Civil liberties are those fundamental values not explicitly protected by the Constitution but which the Supreme Court has protected against government infringement. Many personal rights, referred to collectively as the "right" to privacy, for example, constitute civil liberties which cannot be found in the Constitution but which exist as the result of court decisions. They are "basic liberties" not tied to or justifiable by a specific constitutional guarantee.

Thoughtful observers of the United States in the nineteenth century worried that Americans would not adequately protect or nourish privacy—what Alexis de Tocqueville called their sense of "private independence." Nonetheless, a surprisingly well-developed system of law on privacy existed by the middle of the century, to protect citizens—mainly white males and their dependents. Jurists regarded individual rights as inseparable from property and liberty, a very limited and literal concept of privacy which, nevertheless, was a major bulwark against censorship. Courts interpreted the First Amendment's expressed guarantees of free speech, press, assembly, and religion so as to protect "private sentiment" and "private judgment," including anonymous or pseudonymous public statements. In addition, they interpreted the Fourth Amendment's "protection of people" in their persons, homes, papers, and effects, against "unreasonable searches and seizures," as insurance against unauthorized disclosure of the contents of personal papers, letters, and telegrams. Privacy rulings also protected juries, legislative committees, and government agencies from having to reveal their proceedings or working papers.

By the time of the Civil War, according to Alan F. Westin, "a republican and libertarian balance had been established among the values of privacy, disclosure, and surveillance." These early juridical interpretations did not assert any "right" of privacy, in the modern pluralistic sense, for those who lived outside of established norms. But for those within mainstream America, the courts seemed well on their way to providing what de Tocqueville thought they should in a democracy: the protection of "private rights and interests . . . to keep pace with the growing equality of conditions."

The balance that had been achieved, by the mid-nineteenth century, between censorship and privacy, was rudely broken, first by the Civil War and then by three technological innovations: the telephone, the microphone (making wiretaps possible), and "instantaneous photography" (as opposed to the original process which required the subject to sit quietly for minutes). From the 1880s to the 1950s the American courts failed to apply the First, Fourth, and Fifth Amendments effectively to technological invasions of personal privacy and privacy of communication, especially when the violation was made by local or state law-enforcement agencies.

Instead, the Supreme Court used these amendments to uphold what Westin has called "propertied privacy." Once the justices declared corporations "persons," and business establishments "homes," all courts protected them from regulation on privacy grounds, including the implicit First Amendment "right of silence," meaning that they did not even have to provide written statements explaining the dismissal of employees. Not until 1937 did New Deal legislation, prompted by the Great Depression, finally end the "propertied privacy" of businesses. Government agencies finally obtained the right to investigate private businesses, on the ground that their transactions affected the public interest. In the process, concepts of what constituted public and private rights began to change, and new questions arose about their relationship.

As late as the 1950s, the Supreme Court still had not decided that individuals retained implicit rights to privacy under the First Amendment. Instead, state courts used common law to protect the privacy of individuals from invasion by photographers, the press, or sound-producing devices. National privacy rights against surveillance techniques developed by state law-enforcement agencies were not upheld until 1949, in *Wolf v. Colorado* (338 U.S. 25 [1949]), and even after this decision evidence obtained from illegal search and seizure, often involving technologically advanced listening devices, continued to be admissible in court.

A constitutional revolution occurred after Earl Warren became chief justice of the U.S. Supreme Court in 1953. During Warren's sixteen-year tenure on the bench, the Court developed an activist approach in many areas, but especially with respect to the establishment of a variety of new personal rights to privacy. One of the Court's decisions involving censorship and privacy rights was *Lopez v. U.S.* (373 U.S. 427 [1963]). In a dissenting opinion that reexamined the entire issue of electronic eavesdropping, Justice William J. Brennan stated:

> Electronic surveillance strikes deeper than at the ancient feeling that a man's home is his castle; it strikes at freedom of communication, a postulate of our kind of society.... [F]reedom of speech is undermined where people fear to speak unconstrainedly in what they suppose to be the privacy of home and office.... The right of privacy is the obverse of freedom of speech in another sense. This Court has lately recognized that the First Amendment freedoms may include the right, under certain circumstances, to anonymity.... Electronic surveillance destroys all anonymity and all privacy; it makes government privy to everything that goes on.

In *Lopez*, Brennan failed to persuade a majority of his colleagues that wiretapping and other forms of electronic surveillance should be put under some kind of judicial control. Various other decisions of the Court, however, beginning with *Mapp v. Ohio* (367 U.S. 643 [1961]), eventually led to the application of the "exclusionary rule" whereby evidence obtained in violation of the Fourth Amendment is not admissible in court.

The Warren Court was to define at least four major privacy rights. The first is the "inviolability of privacy in group association," in a case which the National Association for the Advancement of Colored People brought in 1957 when the State of Alabama tried to obtain its membership lists. The second is the "inviolability of privacy belonging to a citizen's political loyalties" when an individual is questioned by Congress; this right is also known as "political privacy." The third is the "right to anonymity in public expression," and the fourth is the concept of "privacy of the body" or "inviolability of the person." The latter refers to the right of privacy against state interference in personal activities, such as marital and family relationships and matters relating to medical treatment and contraception. The most famous of the contraceptive cases, *Griswold v. Connecticut* (381 U.S. 479 [1965]), enunciated certain "fundamental personal liberties," which include "the right of privacy in the marital relation," under the "liberty" and "due process" clauses of the Fifth and Fourteenth Amendments. The Court's decisions permitting the dissemination and use of contraceptive devices, and proclaiming the "freedom to marry" as a "basic civil right of man," paved the way for the legalization of abortions, in *Roe v. Wade* (410 U.S. 113 [1973]), on the ground that termination of pregnancy is a matter of "private conscience" between a woman and her physician.

Not all Supreme Court justices and other jurists have accepted the idea that a general right to privacy is a fundamental personal liberty implicit in the Bill of Rights. Nevertheless, decisions of the Warren Court have shifted the emphasis with respect to privacy from considerations of property and purely political liberties to personal ones, thus broadening the ways in which privacy rights may be used to protect individuals and groups from physical or intellectual censorship. The more conservative Supreme Court under Chief Justice Warren E. Burger has not, to date, overturned any major Warren Court precedents on privacy—not even the one on abortion.

Both Alexis de Tocqueville and George Orwell believed that, in a functioning democracy, individual expression and privacy were intercon-

▼ **The Arrest of Margaret Sanger.** 1916. Photograph. When Sanger and two other women opened a birth-control clinic in the Brownsville section of Brooklyn in 1916, a policewoman posing as a client came to be fitted for a diaphragm. This photograph shows Sanger being led off to jail by law officers. *Ex. no. 218*

◄ **The Woman Rebel.** September-October 1914. Margaret Sanger edited this feminist newspaper, which advocated the practice of birth control. After five issues it was suppressed by the Post Office. *Ex. no. 215*

nected mainstays of full humanity. De Tocqueville's fears about privacy rights in the United States were unfounded. But his concern that free expression might suffer erosion through the debasing effect of mass politics, with its tendency to devalue language, remains far from allayed. The United States has already experienced some such erosion, in part because of what Herbert Marcuse has called "repressive tolerance" by the state; that is, allowing but not listening to dissenting opinions. It has also occurred through what Conor Cruise O'Brien has called "counterrevolutionary subordination"; that is, saying what the government wants to hear, in return for remuneration and status, or saying nothing in return for the minimum material security provided by the welfare state. Orwell saw this same erosion of free speech being justified in the name of national security during a condition of perpetual war or preparation for war. In fact, in his book *1984*, he developed "newspeak," an entirely debased language many of whose acronyms and sanitized terms sound disturbingly like contemporary military or computer jargon.

Unfortunately, the prophecies of both de Tocqueville and Orwell about the survival of free expression may prove to be more accurate than we care to think. Until World War I, in the United States, abridgement of free speech usually came from state or local, rather than federal agencies. Despite the common law principle of seditious libel, popular belief in freedom of expression remained strong throughout the early nineteenth century. The subtle limitations that existed arose from the homogeneous nature of American society and the commonly held assumptions about essential values. In the more turbulent, more diverse cultural and intellectual atmosphere that developed during the three decades before the Civil War, however, some states, especially those in the South, concerned about rising abolitionist sentiment, began passing laws to control speech, press, and discussion. Throughout the nineteenth and early twentieth centuries, moreover, there were local eruptions of censorship arising from nativist outbursts against various groups that were not in the mainstream of American life—Mormons, Jews, blacks, Catholics, American Indians, and immigrants. The aim of these outbursts was not to stamp out the offending persons or groups, however, so much as to pressure them to conform to prevailing conventions. The relatively limited contact between Americans of different socioeconomic backgrounds provided some restraint on the spread of organized censorship. For most of the nineteenth century, accordingly, censorship was local in scope, specific to class, and non-ideological.

Not until early in the twentieth century, when nativist political action united with anti-socialist and anti-communist ideologies, did the societal restraints on censorship begin to lessen. By that time, the United States had been transformed from a primarily agricultural and rural nation to the world's greatest center of industry and commerce. Immigration and intermarriage were making the population increasingly diverse, while the American penchant for mobility began to weaken the traditional bonds of local society. Simultaneously, the development of certain kinds of conflict that seemed to affect the entire nation—workers' strikes, suspected anarchist plots, and then World War I—engaged the federal government as a party to the effort to preserve social and cultural order. The federal concern was reflected in the Defense Secrets Act of 1911, the Espionage Act of 1917, and the Sedition Act of 1918.

Free speech is always an early casualty of war—both during and following the period of armed hostility. World War I set major censorship prece-

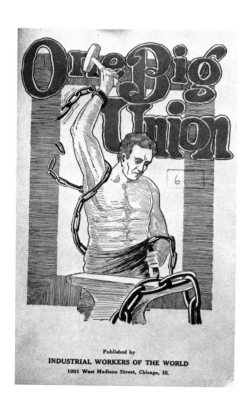

▼ **One Big Union.** Ca. 1915. The International Workers of the World (I.W.W.) printed pamphlets like this to take their message to the working classes. In response, vigilante groups organized in various parts of the country to suppress the activities and publications of the union. *Ex. no. 221*

dents which continue to haunt Americans. While the Committee on Public Information worked to unite American opinion behind the Allied powers fighting Germany, the Espionage Act was used not simply to punish spies and saboteurs, but also to eliminate all opposition to the war, especially among radical labor groups like the International Workers of the World (I.W.W.). Local intolerance and conformism, exacerbated by the emotional patriotism generated (with government approbation) during the war, spilled over into the 1920s, beginning with the Red Scare and restrictions on immigration. Security concerns took precedence over personal liberties and free speech as the Bolshevik Revolution conditioned Americans to accept ideology, instead of culture or morals, as the rationale for controlling action and information. Although the Sedition Amendment to the Espionage Act was repealed in 1921, the rights to free expression and assembly of unions, communist groups, and the unemployed were often not respected during the postwar years.

Not until the early 1930s did the Supreme Court finally rule against state violations of freedom of the press, in *Near v. Minnesota* (283 U.S. 697 [1931]) and *Stromberg v. California* (238 U.S. 359 [1931]). The Supreme Court initially turned its back on violations of workers' rights which employers committed in the name of FDR's "war" against the Great

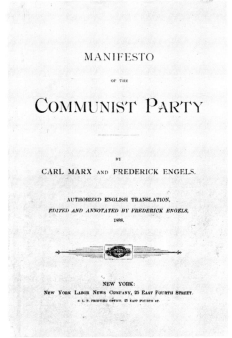

▶ Marx and Engels, **Communist Manifesto.** 1888. Originally published (in German) in London in 1848, the *Manifesto* was immediately banned by the Prussian government following the revolutions of that year. *Ex. no. 233*

▼ Anonymous Russian, **The October Revolution Is a Fight Against the Church and Religion for the Freedom of the Intellect and Science.** 1923. Poster. *Ex. no. 278*

Depression, but by the late 1930s the Court and Congress had reversed the repressive trend which emerged after World War I. Despite assorted security measures, including the creation of the Office of Censorship, during World War II, civil libertarians had generally become convinced that big government, such as had emerged with New Deal bureaucratic structures, was not the major enemy of free expression. Instead, they concentrated their anticensorship efforts on local authorities. The error of this viewpoint soon became evident as the McCarthyite red scare followed soon after the world war, and as the Cold War, with its heavy emphasis on ideology, became a permanent part of life.

Ironically, just when these things were happening, during the late 1940s and early 1950s, intellectual theories about pluralism, dating from the 1920s, began to manifest themselves in practical ways among certain "have-not" groups whose yearnings for greater participation in American society had long been muted and ignored. The intellectual and anthropological case for both cultural pluralism and cultural relativism, in favor of group diversity within a more comprehensive national community, began to be made by thinkers like Horace M. Kallen, Randolph Bourne, Franz Boas, and Ruth Benedict. Their disciples, along with a variety of literary figures, ranging from Sherwood Anderson and William Carlos Williams to D.H. Lawrence, criticized the social and political Americanism of the assimilationists, as well as the social-control theories which many Progressives brought to their reform work among immigrant populations.

Ultimately, growing restiveness among civil-rights, minority, ethnic, and peace groups in the late 1950s and 1960s produced a series of Supreme Court decisions and supportive congressional legislation, including the 1964 Civil Rights Act, which began to acknowledge the legitimate rights and needs of minority peoples and women. Pluralism, no longer simply the utopian dream of a small group of intellectuals, had come to mean the legitimization of cultural diversity.

Alas, the heyday of pluralism proved more short-lived than even its most confirmed enemies had predicted. By 1975, after a decade of rapid

▶ **Envelope labeled "Opened by Censor."** 1918. The desire to protect national security in wartime led to a surge of public and government concern about threats from Germany and her supporters in the United States. This envelope is witness to one modest but thoroughly implemented procedure—censorship of mail from abroad. *Ex. no. 227*

(No. 1)

cultural and political shocks, many Americans had decided that pluralism had gone far enough. The humiliating end to the Vietnam War provoked a stronger conservative backlash than had followed either world war. Watergate, after stirring up great debate about deep constitutional issues, including privacy, lost prominence as a new political agenda fostered more rather than less secretiveness in government. The fiscal demands of the war and the Great Society finally caught up with the economy, to create, by the late 1970s, both high inflation and high unemployment. An avalanche of reaction blocked further attempts at federal action in support of civil-liberties issues such as busing, abortion, the Equal Rights Amendment, affirmative action, obscenity, and gay rights. The popular mood fixated on a return to the "good old days" of a mythical past. One way to achieve this return was to censor new ideas and the groups or individuals associated with them.

Today, the general public seems more willing to support a wide variety of censorship than at any time since the 1920s. At the local and state levels the most characteristic expression of this willingness is the epidemic of attempts to censor books and films in the schools. During the early 1970s, approximately one hundred book-banning incidents occurred, according to the American Library Association's Office for Intellectual Freedom; by the late 1970s that number had tripled; and by 1981 there were over nine hundred reported cases of attempts to ban books in primary and secondary schools across the country. In 1982 a national survey of 860 school librarians revealed that thirty-four percent had encountered challenges to books on their shelves. Over half of these resulted in the removal of a contested book. One can only imagine how much self-censorship of books results from community pressure, without benefit of litigation and thus without arousing much public attention or concern.

Films have also been subjected to numerous attacks by censors. Unlike printed material, however, movies did not receive constitutional protection as a form of free expression until 1952. Before then, they were subjected to censorship by such myriad local, state, and federal representatives as customs officials, attorneys, mayors, governors, librarians, teachers, fire, safety, and health board members, and of course by police officers. While countless films have probably been privately censored,

◀ Art Young, **The Hand That Rocks the Cradle.** Ca. 1914. Pendrawing. *Ex. no. 245*

fewer have been publicly banned. Not surprisingly, the most extensive public debate and legal discussion of film censorship occurred in the 1960s and early 1970s, the period of intense civil-rights and antiwar activity. After a generally liberalizing trend in the direction of less censorship, changes in plurality and majority decisions of the Supreme Court now point in the direction of more rather than less official censorship. The court decided, in *Miller v. California* (431 U.S. 15 [1973]), that community rather than national standards should determine whether or not a work is obscene. This decision has encouraged local juries to make their own determinations about the "literary, artistic, political, or scientific" values of works standing accused of obscenity.

The most disturbing feature of the current rise in censorship is the encouragement it has received from the executive branch of the federal government, through the control of information in the name of internal and external security. Throughout the twentieth century, federal restraints on expression have assumed many overt forms: anti-anarchist legislation, sedition laws, denaturalization, injunctions, deportation, registration of politically suspect groups, loyalty oaths, security checks, and clearance classifications for those handling sensitive materials. In addition, a system of covert or "shadow" procedures for gathering and controlling information has emerged. The FBI, since its formation in 1907, has assumed responsibility for protecting internal security through domestic intelligence, while the CIA, founded in 1947, primarily provides information about foreign intelligence to protect national security.

Increasingly during the Cold War years, both agencies have engaged in extralegal and clandestine activity, with or without the knowledge of top government officials, in their pursuit of subversives. During the war in Vietnam, under the Johnson administration, the CIA established a special domestic unit called Operation CHAOS for determining whether antiwar groups were financed by foreign enemies of the United States. Under Nixon's first administration an elaborate plan was developed, but never implemented, for coordinating all counterintelligence agencies from the Army, Navy, Air Force, CIA, and FBI into an Interagency Group on Domestic Intelligence and Internal Security. The Nixon administration employed surveillance tactics against domestic antiwar and other protest groups through a variety of extralegal means.

Revelations flowing out of Watergate temporarily halted covert federal harassment of counterculture groups but did not end a trend toward growing activity by local law-enforcement agencies. During the 1960s, the FBI, CIA, and many state and local intelligence units had formed links with each other in an attempt to monitor and control the growing movement against the Vietnam War. This decentralized system remained after the war ended, and has been one means through which local communities have assumed more and more authority over the gathering of political intelligence and the censoring of publications and films. Simultaneously, as the global power of the United States seemed to wane during the decades of the Cold War, successive administrations in Washington became ever more interested in the whole issue of access to information, not just information relating to subversion. The decade after Watergate has thus seen an unprecedented convergence of the forces in favor of censorship, in the cause of local determination and domestic or national security.

This development has confounded both civil libertarians and political reformers. Initially, Watergate revelations and subsequent government reforms, including the Freedom of Information and the Privacy Acts, encouraged civil libertarians to think that the system could, indeed, expand freedoms and protect itself from abuse of power at all levels. Their optimism soon faded, as reform efforts either failed or produced unanticipated problems. For example, in 1973 Congress attempted, through the War Powers Act, to limit presidential authority to commit troops abroad. Despite this act, Congress has found it extremely difficult to impose its will on the presidency—Lebanon and Grenada being two recent cases—and the whole validity of the act has been called into question by a 1983 Supreme Court Decision on legislative vetoes. Again, during the 1970s, Congress passed legislation that limited the size of individual contributions to political campaigns. The result, ironically, has been to encourage the creation of political action committees (PACs), which have been used with great effect by various special-interest groups.

Moreover, government actions threaten to impair the liberalizing effect of the 1974 amendments to the Freedom of Information Act (FOIA) and of the Privacy Act. When the Reagan administration took office, even the strongest opponents of the FOIA, such as Senator Orrin Hatch, agreed that the intent of Congress in establishing the law in 1966, and in amending it, was to "empower individuals to hold government accountable for its use of sensitive information," and to communicate necessary government information to the electorate. Deputy Attorney General of the U.S. Edward C. Schmults said, in a speech in 1981, that Congress "sought to insure that our citizens would be permitted to discover what records the government keeps on them and how that information . . . would be used." Nevertheless, the past three years have seen many attempts to increase the number of exemptions to the FOIA, and to use the Privacy Act as a means of restricting public access to information instead of as a means of limiting the flow of personal information to protect individuals from unwarranted disclosure.

Related to access to information is the right of the executive branch to classify government documents as secret. This right was assumed as early as the presidency of George Washington, but formal regulations protecting the secrecy of sensitive information did not appear until 1869. Not until shortly before World War II did the government create a full-fledged system of classifying confidential material. FDR's Executive Order 8381 (1940), which covered all national defense matters, was based on a 1938 statute concerning the security of armed-forces installations and equipment. In 1951, President Truman issued the first executive order (10104) that extended secrecy procedures, in the name of national security, to all civilian departments. Subsequent presidents have issued similar executive orders. President Reagan's Order 12356 (1982) is the most restrictive because it requires the classification of more material than is strictly necessary to protect domestic national security. Congressman Glenn English, chair of the Subcommittee on Government Information and Individual Rights, called the Reagan approach "a return to the days when 'national security' was used by bureaucrats and politicians to hide errors, mistakes, and waste." English characterized this as "part of a pattern of the Reagan Administration efforts to cut back on the public's right to know what is going on in the government."

In fact, secrecy seems to have become a synonym for security. In 1983, the Reagan administration proposed, in "National Security Decision Directive 84," lifelong review of books and speeches written by former government officials who had access to classified information (including, presumably, former presidents), and lie detector tests for those suspected of leaking sensitive government information. Although this Orwellian-titled attempt at presidential censorship has been partly withdrawn, the sentiment it represents may perhaps weaken current judicial or legislative safeguards against excessive government secrecy.

Directive 84 is one of many recent attempts by the federal government to put less emphasis on enforcing civil-rights legislation and protecting the privacy of citizens. Others include contingency plans for dealing with domestic and international terrorism; the reversal of a policy, begun under the Nixon administration, that forbade racially segregated schools from enjoying federal tax exemptions; and a reluctance to enforce federal laws against discrimination in housing and education. The attempts also include efforts to pass a school-prayer amendment, and legal actions by the Justice Department against the parents of malformed children, against the establishment of comparable pay for women (in Washington State), and against access to abortion. All of these attempts have been justified as necessary to restore proper balance to the relationship between local authorities and the national government, according to the principles of the New Federalism.

Many dissenting voices have been raised against these efforts to limit rights or slow the enforcement of rights. George Reedy, former press secretary under President Johnson, testified in February 1984 before the House Subcommittee on Civil Service about the futility of the secrecy approach contained in Directive 84:

> In our nation, the obsession with secrecy... seems to have arisen out of our awe concerning the marvels of modern technology. This, in my judgment, is an illogical reaction. One of the offshoots of modern technology is the virtual abolition of any possibility of secrecy. This disturbing reality—disturbing because technology is abolishing personal as well as national privacy—does not seem to be comprehended by the ruling elements of our society. Many of our political leaders are still living in the past on this issue of security. They are under the illusion that somewhere long-haired "scientists" with cracked microscopes are twiddling dials in suburban basements and that the right twiddle will somehow produce a death ray which will keep us from all harm as long as no one else stumbles across the "secret." This is not a comprehension of science, engineering and technology. It is a belief in 20th-century witchcraft. Unfortunately, it is a belief that results in frantic efforts to maintain something called "security." They are efforts to exorcise demons which are on the same level as the amulets and incantations employed by our ancestors to ward off banshees, werewolves and "things that go bump in the night...."

There is nothing wrong with taking precautions for national security or with the New Federalism, as long as they do not become pretexts for Big Brotherism. The danger comes from the tendency, in many industrially advanced countries, of the citizens to prefer material comfort and national security to civil rights and liberties, and to accept government-prescribed codes of behavior, especially during times of stress. In the United States this tendency began to appear with the New Deal and the Second World War, when government guarantees of at least a minimal level of material comfort were followed by massive federal action in all areas of life. Once the federal government became guarantor of last resort for individual material security, as well as for protecting individual civil rights, it acquired control over two often competing social goods, and became capable of exerting a subtle but profound control over life. Traditionally, in the United States, the independence of local institutions has been a principal defense against excesses by the national government, and in theory the New Federalism will restore this defense to its former vigor. But in fact the interpenetration of local and national governments, as seen in the renewed willingness to censor, may be undermining the very strength that is needed at the local level. We may actually be on the verge of fulfilling a prophecy made by de Tocqueville in 1835:

> Subjection in minor affairs breaks out every day, and is felt by the whole community indiscriminately. It does not drive men to resistance, but it crosses them at every turn, till they are led to surrender the exercise of their own will. Thus their spirit is gradually broken and their character enervated.... It is in vain to summon a people, who have been so rendered dependent on the central power, to choose from time to time the representatives of that power; this rare and brief exercise of their free choice, however important it may be, will not prevent them from gradually losing the faculties of thinking, feeling and acting for themselves, and thus gradually falling below the level of humanity.

Once we have accepted interlocking local and federal censorship of speech, information, and actions, can we long avoid losing other civil liberties, in the name of secrecy and security?

SOURCES

In addition to major Supreme Court decisions cited in the text; hearings before the House Subcommittee on Government Information and Individual Rights of the Committee on Government Operations, relating to security classification policy; executive orders; and the Freedom of Information Act, I relied heavily on the proceedings of the Senate Select Committee on Intelligence concerning requests by the CIA and FBI for obtaining further exemptions from the FOIA, and the hearings of the House Subcommittee on Civil Service of the Committee on the Post Office and Civil Service concerning the Reagan administration's National Security Decision Directive 84.

I have also found useful a number of books and articles. On cultural and political history: F. H. Matthews, "The Revolt against Americanism: Cultural Pluralism and Cultural Relativism as an Ideology of Liberation" (*The Canadian Review of American Studies*, vol. 1, 1970, pp. 4-31); Paul Johnson, *Modern Times: The World from the Twenties to the Eighties* (New York: Harper & Row, 1983); Joan Hoff-Wilson, *The Twenties: The Critical Issues* (Boston: Little Brown and Co., 1972); and Sissela Bok, *Lying: Moral Choice in Public and Private Life* (New York: Pantheon Books, 1978). On the history of censorship: David M. Rabban, "The First Amendment in Its Forgotten Years" (*Yale Law Review*, vol. 90, 1981, pp. 522-595); Mark Conrad, "Censorship in America" (*Human Rights*, vol. 10, 1982, pp. 28-31); Edward de Grazia, *Censorship Landmarks* (New York: R.R. Bowker Company, 1969); Charles H. Busha, ed., *An Intellectual Freedom Primer* (Littleton, Colorado: Libraries Unlimited, Inc., 1977); Robert A. Liston, *The Right to Know: Censorship in America* (New York: Franklin Watts, Inc., 1973); Alan F. Westin, *Privacy and Freedom* (New York: Atheneum, 1967).

For First Amendment issues: John Kamp, "Obscenity and the Supreme Court: A Communication Approach to a Persistent Judicial Problem" (*Communications and the Law*, vol. 2, 1980, pp. 1-42); Paul L. Murphy, *The Meaning of Freedom of Speech: First Amendment Freedoms from Wilson to FDR* (Westport, Connecticut: Greenwood Press, 1972); Frances Fitzgerald, "A Reporter at Large (Banned Books)" (*The New Yorker*, January 16, 1984, pp. 47ff). Two articles for which the authors are not indicated are relevant to the issue of government secrecy and surveillance: "Government Information and the Right of Citizens" (*Michigan Law Review*, vol. 73, 1975, pp. 971-1303) and "The Privacy Act of 1974: An Overview" (*Duke Law Review*, 1976, pp. 301-329). In addition, see: K.G. Robertson, *Public Secrets: A Study in the Development of Government Secrecy* (New York: St. Martin's Press, 1982); David Wise, *The Politics of Lying: Government Deception, Secrecy, and Power* (New York: Random House, 1973); Frank J. Donner, *The Age of Surveillance: The Aims and Methods of America's Political Intelligence System* (New York: Alfred A. Knopf, 1980); Christopher N. Was, M. Elizabeth Smith, and Charles Doyle, *Wiretapping and Electronic Surveillance: Federal and State Statutes* (Washington, D.C.: Congressional Research Service, American Law Division, 1975); Mario Pei, *Double-Speak in America* (New York: Hawthorn Books, Inc., 1973). Also useful are Edward de Grazia and Roger K. Newman, *Banned Films: Movie Censors and the First Amendment* (New York: R. R. Bowker Company, 1982) and Vincent Blasi, *The Burger Court: The Counterrevolution That Wasn't* (New Haven: Yale University Press, 1983).

9

Thoughts on Censorship in the World of 1984

STEPHEN SPENDER

Historically, censorship has been applied by the state, the church, committees set up to be guardians of public morality, and many other bodies. Censors can be appointed by governments to deal with particular activities, for example, newspapers, theater, or cinema. There need be no official censorship at all, but laws against pornography, obscenity, blasphemy, etc., to which members of the public, who consider themselves offended by some work shown or published, may appeal in the courts. Thus on August 8, 1929, there was a case held against the proprietors of a London gallery, in response to a complaint by a detective inspector against their exhibiting paintings by D.H. Lawrence which the detective inspector considered obscene.

Members of an older generation, like myself, remember the time when James Joyce's *Ulysses* was banned. When I was an Oxford undergraduate, if one went to Paris during the vacation and bought at Sylvia Beach's famous bookshop Shakespeare and Cie. a copy of *Ulysses* and attempted to smuggle it through the customs at Dover, one might well have one's purchase confiscated and have to pay a fine for being in possession of a notorious work of pornography.

To many English today, mention of censorship will bring to mind what is commonly referred to as the "trial of Lady Chatterley"—as though the heroine of D.H. Lawrence's novel *Lady Chatterley's Lover* were herself on trial—an idea that would have appealed to Lawrence. Censorship pro-

STEPHEN SPENDER printed his first book of poems with his own letterpress in 1933. Over the past five decades he has become widely known as a poet, writer, journalist, editor, and spokesman for the political Left. In trips to Europe, the Middle East, and North America he has lectured on poetry and modern English; he has held visiting professorships at many universities in the United States. In 1965 he became the first non-U.S. citizen ever to be appointed Overseas Consultant in Poetry and English to the Library of Congress.

Stephen Spender's long interest in human rights led him, in 1968, to help found the *Index on Censorship*, which is published regularly as an advocate of free expression throughout the world. In addition to poetry, literary criticism, translations, and essays, he has published an autobiography, *World Within World* (New York: Harcourt Brace Jovanovich, 1951), and contributed an essay to *The God That Failed: Six Studies in Communism*, edited by Richard Crossman (New York: Harper & Row, 1950). His current projects include a translation of the *Oedipus* trilogy and a second autobiography.

B. W. HUEBSCH, Inc., *Publisher,* 116 WEST 13TH STREET

Office of THE FREEMAN

CABLES: YEARBOOK NEWYORK
TELEPHONES: 2988-9 WATKINS

NEW YORK CITY
April 5, 1921

Mr. John Quinn
31 Nassau Street
New York City

Dear Mr. Quinn,

    In accordance with your telephone request I send you this note to confirm my attitude toward Joyce's "Ulysses".

    A New York court having held that the publication of a part of this in the Little Review was a violation of the law, I am unwilling to publish the book unless some changes are made in the manuscript as submitted to me by Miss H. S. Weaver who represents Joyce in London.

    In view of your statement that Joyce declines absolutely to make any alterations, I must decline to publish it. I repeat, however, that if you or Joyce, or both, conclude that a change of some kind in the manuscript is desirable, I feel that I am entitled to the first offer of the American rights under those circumstances.

    At your request I send herewith the manuscript of the book exactly in the shape as it was delivered to me by Miss Weaver in London. My understanding with her was that I should return the book to her if I do not publish it, so strictly speaking, I am violating that understanding by sending it to you. Under the circumstances, I would thank you to send me an acknowledgment which will entirely absolve me, so that I may set myself straight with Miss Weaver.

    Very truly yours,

BWH:LB

enc.

voked Lawrence into writing in 1929 a pamphlet entitled *Pornography and Obscenity*. In the concluding pages of this, he makes some observations going far beyond the particular matter of pornography into the wider issue of individual freedom:

> If my individual life is to be enclosed within the huge corrupt lie of society today, purity and the dirty little secret, then it is worth not much to me. Freedom is a very great reality. But it means, above all things, freedom from lies. It is first, freedom from myself, from the lie of myself, from the lie of my all-importance, even to myself; it is freedom from the self-conscious masturbating thing I am, self-enclosed. And second, freedom from the vast lie of the social world, the lie of purity and the dirty little secret. All the other monstrous lies lurk under the cloak of this one primary lie. The monstrous lie of money lurks under the cloak of purity. Kill the purity-lie and the money-lie will be defenseless.

English and Americans today probably connect censorship—or rather the lack of it—with the immense increase in the numbers of books, magazines, films, and video concerned with sex and violence. Some of them may ask, "Should there be total freedom of expression for those who exploit a huge commercial market?" Lawrence would not have thought so. He wrote in the essay quoted above:

> But even I would censor genuine pornography, rigorously. It would not be very difficult. In the first place, genuine pornography is almost always underworld. It doesn't come into the open. In the second, you can recognize it by the insult it offers, invariably, to sex, and to the human spirit.
>
> Pornography is the attempt to insult sex, to do dirt on it. This is unpardonable.

One suspects that Lawrence would have been quite happy to see James Joyce and Henry Miller censored, both of whom he would have considered to be "doing dirt on sex." He certainly would have been horrified at the enormous outpouring, from all the sewers of the underworld, of pornography, following on the acquittal of Lady Chatterley.

For most people in the West today the word pornography probably suggests what is grotesquely called "adult literature." If they have misgivings about such works, this will probably be because they fear that reading them might harm some, if not all, of those subjected to their influence. In answer to these misgivings, many writers would argue (I have heard them do so at writers' conferences) that literature cannot have a bad influence on readers. There seem to be elements of Orwellian doublethink in this argument, for the same writers who put it forward would certainly claim that, in every other respect, their writings were influential.

Perhaps the strongest argument against censorship of the novel was put forward by Henry James in 1884 in *The Art of Fiction*. Attacking Walter Besant who had, in that year, delivered an address at the Royal Institution, in which he congratulated contemporary English fiction for its morality (by which he meant its failure to discuss sexual relations), James wrote:

> In the English novel (by which of course I mean the American as well), more than in any other, there is a traditional difference between that which people know and that which they agree to

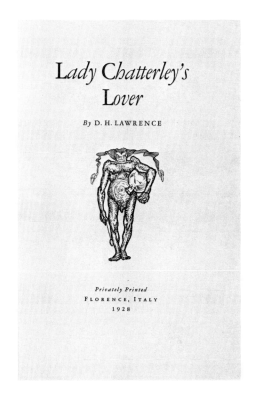

▲ D.H. Lawrence, **Lady Chatterley's Lover.** 1928. Copies of the first edition of *Lady Chatterley*, privately printed by Lawrence in Italy, were seized whenever discovered by customs agents in England and the United States. *Ex. no. 254*

◄ **Letter of B.W. Huebsch to John Quinn.** April 5, 1921. James Joyce refused to make the deletions that Huebsch sought. *Ex. no. 249*

admit that they know, that which they see and that which they speak of, that which they feel to be a part of life and that which they allow to enter literature. There is the great difference, in short, between what they talk of in conversation and in print.

He responds with crushing finality to Walter Besant:

> The essence of moral energy is to survey the whole field, and I should directly reverse Mr. Besant's remark and say not that the English novel has a purpose, but that it has a diffidence. To what degree a purpose in a work of art is a source of corruption I shall not attempt to inquire; the one that seems to me least dangerous is the purpose of making a perfect work. As for our novel, I may say lastly on this score that as we find it in England today it strikes me as addressed in a large degree to "young people," and that this in itself constitutes a presumption that it will be rather shy.

I should not presume to guess that this puts Henry James on the side of what Lawrence calls "the underworld." But it does mean that James thought that the literary artist should be able, in his art, to transform material of life which covers the whole range of human experience. To say that he should not touch on certain "dirty" aspects of it is like saying that a doctor should not operate on certain parts of the body, or a psychoanalyst discuss certain areas of neurosis, because they are unmentionable and, if activated, probably immoral. James Joyce, in saying that he intended to write, in *Ulysses*, about the "whole of life" was like a physiologist of earlier times who, when the church banned dissection of corpses, claimed the right to find out everything about human anatomy.

But the penalty of making it possible to publish literature about every aspect of human experience is that many writers will and do write what Lawrence objected to as "genuine pornography," that which he would have been the first to censor.

▲ Max Beckmann, **Adam and Eve.** 1917. Etching. *Ex. no. 236*

▶ Jean Genêt, **Querelle de Brest.** 1947. For many years this privately printed edition was an underground classic. The illustrations were by Jean Cocteau. *Ex. no. 256*

Since the 1950s, poets and novelists writing about every possible extreme of exploration by the individual of his own physical and mental individuality seem to have approached some absolute of freedom. For the serious writer, the problem of censorship is superseded by the problem of how to use and not abuse freedom at a time when the immense pressure of the market is brought on writers to publish what thirty years ago would have been made unpublishable by the laws regarding obscenity. Lawrence's remark, quoted above, that the "monstrous lie of money lurks under the cloak of purity" is now replaced by another: "the monstrous lie of money now demands the pornographic which lurks under the cloak of truth." The pressure of the market now might be described as a kind of censorship in reverse.

One result of this is to widen the gap between what is privately revelatory or confessional—where there is total freedom—and what may be written about matters of public interest. Here there is still the kind of old-fashioned unstated censorship imposed by pressure groups and commercial interests. What goes and does not go into newspapers is subject to an unstated censorship arising from the views of newspaper proprietors, the concern of advertisers and even, recently in England, of the leaders of trade unions whose members print the newspapers. There are also stringent laws protecting official secrets, and other laws regarding the length of time that must pass before official documents may be published. A bizarre example of censorship not called by that name is the recent revelation of the fact that the seriousness of Winston Churchill's illness, when he had a stroke during his last premiership, was concealed from the British public by the government with the collusion of editors. As Humbert Wolfe put it:

> You cannot hope
> to bribe or twist
> thank God! the British journalist.
> But seeing that what man will do
> unbribed, there's no occasion to.

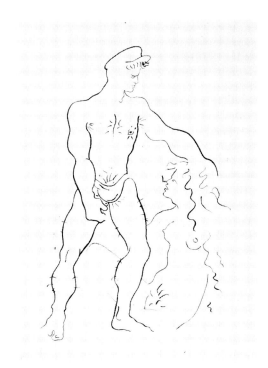
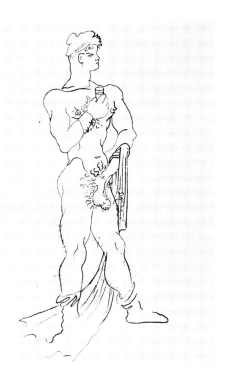

Of course, there is a wide diversity of opinions expressed in the media, but all are liable to reflect the views of the great interests which control them. All are ultimately answerable toward standards of money-making. This means that unorthodox opinions are permitted insofar as they help fill the proprietor's pocket. By this, I do not mean, of course, that they are necessarily excluded if they do not do so. There is much latitude. With the gutter press, where there is cutthroat competition between newspapers to obtain the largest number of readers, in the war-to-the-death for circulation, nearly everything except the news is reduced to the same level of triviality, diversified with pornography—a word which, as these newspapers amply show, rhymes with "photography."

In the late 1960s and during the 1970s in America there was a generation of great poets who, although highly individualistic in their writing, felt tragically cut off from terrible realities of American public life (for example, the war in Vietnam) which cast shadows on their work while at the same time their poetry and criticism left not the slightest trace on American public life. The poets I am thinking of were Robert Lowell, John Berryman, Theodore Roethke, and Randall Jarrell, all of whose lives ended rather tragically. These poets had the sense of living out in their imaginations a tragedy whose nature they, above all others, realized, but in which they were, as voices of the imagination, unheard. I once heard Robert Lowell observe to the Russian poet Andreï Voznesenski that he could almost envy Russian poets for living in a country where the government took them seriously enough to send them to prison and ban their books. At the time I could not help thinking that this was rather like hearing a millionaire say to a beggar that he envied him for starving because it brought him down to the basic realities of food. Yet I could understand Lowell's bitterness. Some years later, on English TV, when Joseph Brodsky had put to him the question of whether he did not prefer the seriousness with which the Russian authorities took poets to the indifference with which the American authorities treated them, he replied: "Yes, I know. But I prefer America." It was the answer of someone who had had reason to reflect about the matter.

Freedom of expression may be imperfect in the West, and frustrated by all sorts of restrictions and inhibitions, even by corruption. But the difference between censorship in the West and in the communist countries is so great that it amounts, not to a difference of degree, but of kind.

We fail sometimes to realize this because we think of censorship principally as affecting individual writers whose works are banned and who themselves may be harassed, imprisoned, confined to insane asylums. It is indeed important to remember that censorship in totalitarian societies is more than a matter of the persecution of individual writers and other artists. It is a matter of the dictatorship monopolizing all the media of communication with the people, who are told only what the government wants them to know.

In totalitarian societies there are really two aspects of censorship. One is negative—the censoring and repression of the Russian dissident writers, for example. The other is positive: that of the authorities who issue or withhold information, provide censored reports of events, and make propaganda. Since the authorities are in control of the society and since the dissidents are only voices crying in the wilderness, what I call positive censorship characterizes the society much more than negative censorship.

The fact of there being centralized governmental censorship in one part of the world and not in another inevitably divides the world into two areas: one, where there is (comparative) freedom of expression, and the other, where there is no such freedom. The effect of this division is, quite inevitably, to distort all relations, political and cultural, between the two world-areas.

An example very much to the fore today should serve to demonstrate this—the effect of Soviet censorship on the debate about nuclear disarmament. The fact that in Russia people are free to protest against nuclear weapons in the West, but not against those in their own country, prevents the possibility of all the peoples of the world uniting in protest against governments that manufacture and stockpile nuclear weapons. The nuclear disarmers in the West are hamstrung by the fact that their agitation can only be directed against the nuclear policies of the United States and other Western countries. If there were a worldwide movement of all peoples against all governments that have nuclear arms the situation would be entirely different. It is difficult to believe that, in such circumstances, the superpowers would not be obliged to give way to what must surely be the devout wish of eighty percent of the population of the world that nuclear weapons should be abolished. As things are, it is the Soviet censorship of freedom of expression which forces the American and Russian governments into macabre collusion in competing with one another for equality, if not superiority, of nuclear-arms power.

Positive censorship is the absolutely indispensable preliminary to dictatorship. This was evident in 1933 when Hitler, on seizing power,

▲   George Grosz, **"Poor hare! Thou playest but a sorry part in this world's drama, but your worshipful lords must needs have hares!"** 1922. Photo lithograph. *Ex. no. 283*

◀   Emil Nolde, **Young Couple.** 1917. Woodcut. The Nazis declared Nolde a "decadent artist." *Ex. no. 235*

МОНАСТЫРСКОЕ „ЖИТИЕ"

На что шли доходы монастырей? На сытую, веселую жизнь братии, на роскошную жизнь „князей церкви", высшего монашества.

О том, как „бражничают" монахи, видно из описания „иноческого жития" в знаменитой Троице-Сергиевой лавре в конце XVIII века.

Эта лавра всегда славилась своими медами, пивами и квасом. Виноградные вина запасались бочками. Каждому монаху ежедневно выдавалась приличная порция „утешительного": бутылка хорошего кагора (виноградное вино), штоф пенного пива и по кувшину меду, пива и кваса. Только в монашескую утробу и можно было ежедневно вливать столько хмельного пойла.

Архимандрит лавры даже в баню ездил в карете, запряженной шестеркой лошадей. Впереди кареты ехал дьякон в стихаре с посохом, а позади телега с различными припасами. Пол в бане устилали пахучими травами и цветами, поддавали на каменку венгерским вином: этим же вином и окачивался отец архимандрит.

Соборные старцы и настоятели лавры ходили в бархатных и шелковых рясах, в шелковых чулках.

Вот куда шли доходы монастыря и те пожертвования, которые со всех концов России верующий народ приносил в лавру.

▲ Anonymous Russian, **Monastery Life.** 1923. Poster. The low rate of literacy in post-revolutionary Russia made printed images important in the dissemination of government policy and communist ideology. This poster is from a set of seventy that attacked the traditional role of religion in Russia.
Ex. no. 277

▶ **Anti-Nazi Pamphlets.** 1940-45. Propaganda against the Hitler regime was smuggled into the Reich, often disguised in various forms. Clockwise from top left: pudding packet, booklet of cooking recipes, game, tea packet, and leaflet. *New York Public Library: Rare Books and Manuscripts.*

imposed censorship on the entire German press and silenced all political opposition. By dissolving all the socialist and pacifist organizations in Germany, he effectively made socialists and pacifists in England who supported disarmament into becoming, against their own principles and wishes, his assistants in rearming Germany in preparation for his plans to dominate Europe. It is surely no exaggeration to say that if there had been no censorship imposed on Germany in 1933 there would have been no dictatorship, no German rearmament—no war. And if today the people of the world everywhere enjoyed free speech, there would be hope for the future of the world which few thoughtful people (in those countries where they are free to have such thoughts) believe in now. Governmental censorship involves more than censoring those writers and intellectuals who are the dissidents. It involves censoring the whole people, dividing the world into the free and un-free, and thereby inhibiting the development and expression of world opinion regarding the greatest threat to the future—that of nuclear war.

◇   ◇   ◇   ◇

Now it is 1984 and everyone is looking to Orwell's nightmare for prophetic clues to our present situation. What concerns me here is Orwell's insight into the logical extension into the future—us—of Stalinist dictatorship with its extensive machinery of propaganda, police, espionage, and terror—forms of universal censorship capable, as Orwell thought, of being extended to the whole world.

The theoretical basis of Orwell's nightmare of a world divided into three dictatorships is provided in the novel by extracts from a book, secretly circulated among Inner Party Members, and written by one Emmanuel Goldstein (obviously, Trotsky), called *The Theory and Practice of Oligarchic Collectivism*. In formulating this theory, Orwell reveals his fascination with the Soviet trials of the 1930s, in which loyal party members were conditioned by scientific methods to confess to crimes it is inconceivable that they could have committed. He saw the connection between these confessions and the rewriting of entries in the *Soviet Encyclopedia* in order to suppress and distort the historic role of Trotsky in the Revolution. He was impressed also by the "doctoring" of photographs of historic importance—taking out the figures of former revolutionary leaders who had become "non-persons" and, conversely, introducing figures of leaders now established—faking a photograph of a convivial meeting between Lenin and Stalin, for example. Other features of Oceania were suggested by Orwell's experiences in Spain during the Civil War and by wartime London, where the Ministry of Propaganda was called the Ministry of Information, suggesting the Ministry of Truth—for fabricating historic lies—in which Orwell's hero, Winston Smith, is employed.

The central theme of *1984* is the absolute corruption of truth, as perceived by individuals, by the political dictatorship presided over by Big Brother. The wills and lives of individuals merge into the will and policies of the dictatorship. There are passages of *1984* which read like a secular version of Dante's *Divine Comedy*, where all souls are related by proximity to or distance from the will of God, or Big Brother. In his book, Goldstein writes:

> The two aims of the Party are to conquer the whole surface of the earth and to extinguish once and for all the possibility of independent thought. There are therefore two great problems which the Party is resolved to solve. One is to discover, against his will, what another human being is thinking and the other is how to kill several hundred people in a few seconds without giving warning beforehand.

The total destruction of the individual's capacity for independent thought is essential: all other aims are dependent on that. Oceania (or Eurasia, or Eastasia—for their systems are identical) is a mental prison in which the individual is enclosed at every moment within the exigencies of that moment, conforming with party policy. It contains the past only as rewritten to suit the present state of the party. In effect, there is no past, only a continuous present of the party policy. And the future is simply the extension of that policy using the powers of positive censorship to force every mind along its line.

The pressure of the state under the party leadership bears with crushing weight on the mind of every individual capable of thought, willing his behavior and destroying in him all capacity for criticism, even of making those comparisons which consist of measuring present policy against past precedents. There is no past. Censorship has eliminated history.

Through the technological devices of television—emitting propaganda images and receiving images of the spectator—loudspeakers blaring information, and hidden microphones recording conversation, each citizen, instead of being an element within the society capable of thinking about it, becomes an element *thought by it*. The individual is transformed from positive to negative, from critic to criticized, from observer to observed, from acting to being acted upon. He becomes a mechanical

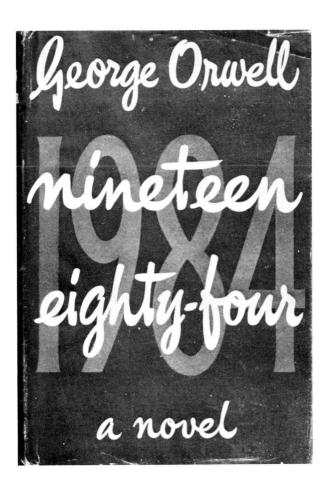

▶ George Orwell, **1984.** 1949. Dustjacket of the first edition. *Ex. no. 276*

receiver for orders bellowed into his ears by loudspeakers—for images of armies and scenes of war imprinted on his eyes by television screens.

There is much in all of this that we would recognize, and there are instruments in our world that seem extrapolated from *1984*, for example, computers with their memories and capacity for storing information about us. All the same, one is brought up against limits of Orwell's imagination, which suggest that *1984* arises perhaps as much from his own illness and depression as it is prophetic of our world and the future beyond it.

One limitation, I think, is his incapacity to imagine a totalitarian society which is not on the Stalinist model. Oceania, Eurasia, and Eastasia are all mirror-images of each other. Yet an American-West European totalitarianism would likely be constructed on a very different model from the Stalinist one. After all, the principle of *1984* is simply that the state must become a highly efficient technological prison in which all the prisoners are reduced more or less to the status of automata. The essential requirement from them is that they hold no critical thoughts about the prison or its warders. Orwell's description shows that so long as they fulfill this desideratum nothing else matters very much. The proles pursue the boisterous activities of a *Lumpenproletariat* without Big Brother's police bothering even to spy on them. And although Orwell's Winston Smith sees promise of revolution coming from them somewhere along the line, this hope does not seem justified within the terms of *1984*.

However, the situation of the proles might suggest the model for another kind of prison. For instance, there might be a prison in which the prisoners were free to write graffiti on the prison walls, write and circulate their own "adult" pornography, smoke pot, paint abstract art, watch videos, and drink large quantities of alcohol without at any moment any of them harboring a thought which threatened Big Brother.

All the mechanics of Orwell's nightmare rely ultimately on the ratio of the immense power of the state to the powerlessness of the individual. Without there being any overt dictatorship, the accumulation of totally disproportionate power by the superpower produces a feeling of powerlessness in the individual. Given the military-industrial complex and a government with immense resources of wealth, maintaining a military posture throughout the world, conducting even—as in *1984*—covert wars with another superpower in an area of the world remote from the center of either of them, the individual is reduced to having only a sense of his own futility. The poem or essay criticizing the state is not even written because the writer realizes it could not have the slightest effect on the surrounding life.

During the Second World War, or just before it, certain French writers—one, I think, was André Gide, another, perhaps, Paul Valéry—took vows of silence, not to write anything about politics until the conflict between powers had resolved itself, for they realized that nothing they wrote could in any way affect events. Self-censorship can arise from a sense of impotence in the face of events.

It is strange that in *1984* there are no dissidents, and indeed nothing of intellectual life. Winston Smith has thoughts but they consist only of awakened memories of the past, sentimental nostalgia combined with a certain stirring of Lawrentian passion for Julia, but without Lawrence's belief that such passion can redeem the world. Perhaps Orwell was so disillusioned by the French and British intellectuals of his time, whom he thought of as selling out to Stalinism, that he failed to notice as part of the Russian phenomenon the survival of a Pasternak. Or perhaps he was really so hypnotized by the power of the police state that, much as he hated it, he could not see beyond it.

The dissidents, however, represent the continuity of intellectual life which in every generation is like a spirit incarnated in certain exceptional individuals. The dissidents in Russia and other places are representative of some continuous, indestructible spirit moving within civilization, which bears witness to qualities intrinsically human, though apparent only in very few human beings in each generation. Here is the disinterested passion for knowledge, for imagination, for recollection of a historic past which can be transmitted to a future and lie germinal within it. The line of intellect has passed through dark ages, cruel persecutions, plagues and natural disasters, terrible wars, our modern Holocaust, and the Gulag Archipelago. The dissidents are not just throwbacks or survivors, freaks of ordinariness like Winston Smith. They are the people who kept little candles alight through all the dark times, recent and long past. Any exhibition about censorship should rank them with the twentieth century's martyrs and heroes.

▼   Kasimir Malevich, **"An Austrian Went to Radziwill and Came Right on to a Peasant Woman's Pitchfork."** 1914-15. Lithograph. Popular Russian World War I propaganda print. *Ex. no. 243*

Шелъ австріецъ въ Радзивилы,
Да попалъ на бабьи вилы.

10

The
Exhibition

The items presented here are organized
in six sections, corresponding to the six
chronological periods of the exhibition.
Within each section, books, pamphlets,
periodicals, and broadsides are listed first,
followed by prints.

Each entry carries an identification
number, which is used also in captions
for those items reproduced in the book.
Within an entry, material enclosed in
square brackets [ ] was obtained through
the Research Libraries catalog of The
New York Public Library. Most entries for
books, pamphlets, and broadsides begin
with the name of the author; items not
easily locatable in the catalog by author's
name are introduced with the appropriate
catalog heading.

In *italics* at the end of each entry
is the name of the Library collection or
division where the work currently resides,
or the name of the lender; and, where
possible to determine, the name of the
donor (if any). Each entry for a print,
in addition, carries the dimensions of
the item in centimeters and (within
parentheses) in inches, with height
preceding width.

I
The Advent and
Expansion of Printing,
1450–1600

1
Apocalypse. French. Illuminated
manuscript, ca. 1280. *Spencer Collection.*

2
Bible. German. 1445. Manuscript. *Rare
Books and Manuscripts.*

3 ▲
Bible. French. **Le Premier (et Le Second)
Volume de la Bible en Francoys.** [Lyon,
Pierre Bailly, 1521] *Rare Books and
Manuscripts.*

4
[Wycliffe Bible] **Bible. New Testament.**
English, manuscript. Ca. 1380. *Rare
Books and Manuscripts.*

5
John Foxe. **The New and Complete Book
of Martyrs.** Vol. 1. New York, William
Durell, 1794. *Rare Books and
Manuscripts.*

6
John Hus. **A Seasonable Vindication of
the Supream Authority and Jurisdiction
of Christian Kings, Lords, and
Parliaments.** London, T. Childe and L.
Parry, 1660. *Rare Books and Manuscripts.*

7
Pope Leo X. **Bulla Contra Errores Martini
Lutheri & Sequacium.** Rome, Jacopo
Mazzocchi, 1520. *Rare Books and
Manuscripts.*

Chꞓiſtus.
Ich müß ouch andern ſtetten predigen das reych gots dan ich
von des wegen geſandt byn vñ hab geprediget yn den Synago/
gen durch Gallileam Luce 4·

8 ▲

Lucas Cranach. **Passional Christi und Antichristi.** Wittenberg, Johann Grunenberg, 1521. *Spencer Collection.*

9

Bible. German. **Biblia, das ist, die gantze Heilige Schrifft Deudsch. Mart. Luth.** Wittenberg, Gedruckt durch Hans Lufft, 1534. 6 v. in 2. *Rare Books and Manuscripts.*

10

Das Babstum mit seynen gliedern gemalet und beschryben gebessert und gemehrt. Nuremberg [Hans Wandereisen? 1526?]. *Spencer Collection.*

11

Martin Luther. **Geystliche Lieder.** Leipzig, Valentin Babst, 1545. *Music Division.*

12 ▲

Hans Sebald Beham. **Biblische Historien figürlich fürbildet.** Frankfurt [1536]. *Spencer Collection.*

13 ▲

[Tyndale Bible] **Bible. New Testament.** English [Antwerp? 1535?]. *Rare Books and Manuscripts.*

14

John Foxe. **The Ecclesiasticall History.** Vol. 2. London, John Daye, 1576. *Rare Books and Manuscripts.*

15

Bible. Latin. Vulgate. **Biblia.** Paris, Robert Stephan, 1528. *Rare Books and Manuscripts.*

16 ▼

John Calvin. **Christianae Religionis Institutio.** Basel, 1536. *Rare Books and Manuscripts.*

17

[Great Bible of Henry VIII] Bible. English. **The Byble in Englyshe.** [London] Rychard Grafton and Edward Whitchurch, 1539. *Rare Books and Manuscripts.*

18

Great Britain. King (Henry VIII). **A Proclamacion, Ordeyned by the Kynges Maiestie, with the Advice of His Honourable Counsayle for the Byble of the Largest and Greatest Volume, to Be Had in Every Churche . . .** London, 1541. *Rare Books and Manuscripts.*

19

Robert Estienne. **Les Censures des Theologiens de Paris.** Paris, Robert Estienne, 1552. *Rare Books and Manuscripts.*

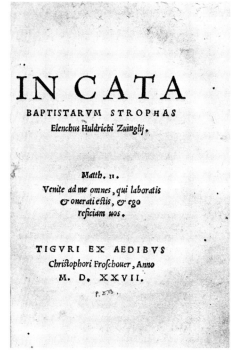

20 ▲

Huldreich Zwingli. **In Catabaptistarum Strophas Elenchus.** Tiguri: Ex Aedibus Christophori Froschouer, 1527. *Rare Books and Manuscripts.*

21

Cochlaeus, i.e., Johannes Dobnek, of Wendelstein. **XXI Articuli Anabaptistarum Monasteriensium.** [Lipsiae?] 1534. *Rare Books and Manuscripts.*

22

Pasquill, of England, pseud. **A Countercuffe Given to Martin Iunior.** [London, John Charlewood?] 1589. *Rare Books and Manuscripts.*

23

Martin Marprelate, pseud. **Oh Read Ouer D. John Bridges, for It Is a Worthy Worke.** [East Molesey, Eng.? Robert Waldegrave, 1588] *Rare Books and Manuscripts.*

24

Catholic Church, Roman. Pope, 1550–1555 (Julius III). **Contra Hebreos Retinentes Libros.** Rome, Antonius Bladus [1554]. *Rare Books and Manuscripts.*

25

Baruch ben Isaac. **Sefer ha-Terumah.** Venice, Daniel Bomberg, 1523. Section from Jewish code of law, written ca. 1200, dealing with idolatry. *Jewish Division, Schiff Collection.*

26

Index Librorum Prohibitorum. **Die Catalogen oft Inventarisen vanden Quaden Verboden Boucken.** Loeuen, Servaes van Sassen, 1550. *Rare Books and Manuscripts.*

27

Council of Trent. **Concilium Tridentinum.** Venice, Hierony. Polum, 1588. *Rare Books and Manuscripts.*

28

Index Librorum Prohibitorum. **Index Auctorum, et Librorum.** Rome, Valerius Doricus, 1559. *Rare Books and Manuscripts.*

29

François Rabelais. **La Plaisante, & Ioyeuse Histoyre du Grand Geant Gargantua.** Valence, Chés Claude La Ville, 1547. *Rare Books and Manuscripts.*

30

Pietro Aretino. **Quattro Comedie.** [London, I. Wolfe] 1588. *Rare Books and Manuscripts.*

31

Desiderius Erasmus. **Moriae Encomium.** [Rotterdam, 1520] *Rare Books and Manuscripts.*

32 ▼

Francesco Colonna. **Hypnerotomachia Poliphili.** Venice, Aldus Manutius, 1499. *Rare Books and Manuscripts.*

33 ▲

Solomon ben Abraham Adret. **Teshuvot she'elot leha-RaSH BA.** Rome, before 1480. Decisions in Jewish law by the leading figure of Spanish Jewry in the late thirteenth century. *Jewish Division, Schiff Collection.*

34 ▼

Catholic Church, Roman. Pope, 1492–1503 (Alexander VI). **[Litterae Indulgentiarum]** [London, Richard Pynson, 1499] *Rare Books and Manuscripts.*

35 ▲

Church of England. **Iniunctions for the Clerge.** [London] 1538. *Rare Books and Manuscripts.*

36
Martin Luther. **Gnade unde frede in Christo.** Wittenberg, 1523. *Rare Books and Manuscripts.*

37
Balthazar Jenichen. **Portrait of Johannes Huss.** 1565. Engraving. 8.6 x 7.2 (3⁷⁄₁₆ x 2¹³⁄₁₆). *Art, Prints and Photographs, Kennedy Fund.*

38 ▲
Balthazar Jenichen. **Portrait of Johannes Calvin.** 1574. Engraving. 8.7 x 7.3 (3⅜ x 2¹⁵⁄₁₆). *Art, Prints and Photographs, Kennedy Fund.*

39
Anonymous German. **Burning Books of the Alexandrian Library.** Folio XCII from Hartmann Schedel's *Nuremberg Chronicle,* Nuremberg, 1493. Woodcut. 14.2 x 10.6 (5⁹⁄₁₆ x 4³⁄₁₆). *Art, Prints and Photographs.*

40
Daniel Hopfer. **Portrait of Martin Luther.** 1523. Etching. 22.8 x 15.2 (9 x 6). *Art, Prints and Photographs, Cadwalader Fund.*

41
Albrecht Altdorfer. **Martin Luther.** 1521. Engraving. 6.0 x 4.0 (2⅜ x 1⁹⁄₁₆). *Art, Prints and Photographs, Kennedy Fund.*

42
Michael Ostendorfer. **Pilgrimage to the Church of the Beautiful Virgin at Ratisbon** (Regensburg). Sixteenth century, before 1559. Woodcut. 54.4 x 38.5 (21⅜ x 15³⁄₁₆). *Art, Prints and Photographs, Kennedy Fund.*

43
Anonymous German? **Luther as a Wolf in the Fold or Luther as a Wolf in Monk's Clothing.** First half, sixteenth century. Engraving. 15.0 x 9.4 (5¹⁵⁄₁₆ x 3¹¹⁄₁₆). *Art, Prints and Photographs, Kennedy Fund.*

44
Anonymous German, after Hans Lautensack. **Evangelium Lucae am xvi Cap.** [or "The Pope as a Rich Man at Table"]. 1562. Engraving. 26.6 x 27.0 (10⁷⁄₁₆ x 10⅝). *Art, Prints and Photographs, Kennedy Fund.*

45
Georg Pencz. **The Rich Man in Hell and Lazarus in Heaven.** Ca. 1542–43. Engraving. 5.9 x 8.5 (2⁵⁄₁₆ x 3⅜). *Art, Prints and Photographs, Kennedy Fund.*

46 ▲
Hans Sebald Beham. **Title page from *Alle Propheten Teutsch.*** Frankfurt, 1534. Woodcuts. 25.5 x 17.5 (10¹⁄₁₆ x 6⅞). *Art, Prints and Photographs, gift of J.S. Morgan.*

47
Wolfgang Stuber. **Luther in His Study.** Late sixteenth century. Engraving. 13.8 x 12.7 (5⁷⁄₁₆ x 5¹⁄₁₆). *Art, Prints and Photographs, Cadwalader Fund.*

48
Albrecht Dürer. **St. Jerome in His Study.** 1514. Engraving. 24.7 x 18.8 (9⅝ x 7⅜). *Art, Prints and Photographs, Kennedy Fund.*

49
Albrecht Dürer. **St. Philip.** 1526 (altered on plate from 1523). Engraving. 12.1 x 7.5 (4¾ x 2¹⁵⁄₁₆). *Art, Prints and Photographs, Samuel Isham Collection.*

50 ▲
Albrecht Dürer. **The Three Peasants.** Probably 1498. Engraving. 10.8 x 7.7 (4¼ x 3). *Art, Prints and Photographs, Samuel Isham Collection.*

51 ▼
Albrecht Dürer. **The Last Supper.** 1523. Woodcut. 21.3 x 30.1 (8⁷⁄₁₆ x 11¹³⁄₁₆). *Art, Prints and Photographs, Kennedy Fund.*

52

Luis de Góngora y Argote. **Soledades.** Madrid, En la Imprenta Real, 1636. *Rare Books and Manuscripts.*

53 ▲

Ivan de Espinosa Medrano. **Apologetico en Favor de D. Luis de Gongora.** Lima, Juan de Queredo y Zarate, 1662. *Rare Books and Manuscripts.*

54 ▼

Juana Ines de la Cruz. **Obras.** Tomo 2. 2d ed. Barcelona, Joseph Llopis, 1693. *Rare Books and Manuscripts.*

55

Galileo Galilei. **Dialogo.** Florence, 1632. *Rare Books and Manuscripts.*

56

Nicolaus Copernicus. **De Revolutionibus Orbium Coelestium.** Nuremberg, 1543. *Rare Books and Manuscripts.*

57

Johann Kepler. **Astronomia Nova.** [Heidelberg, G. Voegelinus] 1609. *Rare Books and Manuscripts.*

58

Index Librorum Prohibitorum. **Index Librorum Prohibitorum Alexandri VII.** Rome, Ex Typographia Reverendae Camarae Apostolicae, 1664. *Rare Books and Manuscripts.*

59

John Toland. **De Genere, Loco, et Tempore Mortis Jordani Bruni Nolani.** London, J. Peele, 1726. *General Research.*

60

Michel de Montaigne. **Essais.** Paris, Chez Abel l'Angelier, 1588. *Rare Books and Manuscripts.*

61

Great Britain. Courts. Court of Star Chamber. **A Decree of Starre-Chamber, Concerning Printing.** Broadside. London, Robert Barker, 1637. *Rare Books and Manuscripts.*

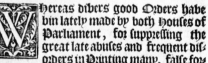

62 ▲

Great Britain. Statutes. **An Order of the Lords and Commons Assembled in Parliament, For the Regulating of Printing.** London, I. Wright, 1643. *Rare Books and Manuscripts.*

63

[Edict of Nantes] **Edict du Roy, & Declaration Sur les Precedents Edicts de Pacification.** Paris, Par les Imprimeurs & Libraires Ordinaires du Roy, 1599. *Rare Books and Manuscripts.*

64
Thomas Hobbes. **Leviathan.** London, Andrew Crooke, 1651. *Rare Books and Manuscripts.*

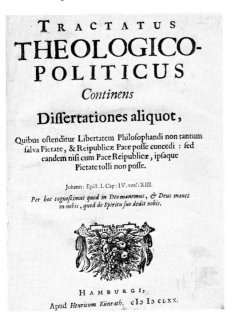

65 ▲
[Benedictus de Spinoza] **Tractatus Theologico-Politicus.** Hamburg, H. Conrad, 1670. *Rare Books and Manuscripts.*

66
John Milton. **Areopagitica.** London, 1644. *Rare Books and Manuscripts.*

67
John Milton. **A Defence of the People of England.** [London] 1692. *Rare Books and Manuscripts.*

68
Great Britain. Crown. By the King. **A Proclamation, for Calling In, and Suppressing of Two Books Written by John Milton.** Broadside. London, John Bill, 1660. *Rare Books and Manuscripts.*

69 ▼
John Milton. **Eikonoklastes in Answer to a Book Intitl'd Eikōn Basilikē.** London, Matthew Simmons, 1649. *Rare Books and Manuscripts.*

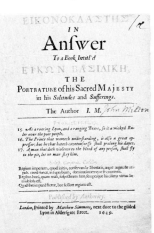

70
John Milton. **The Doctrine & Discipline of Divorce.** London, 1644. *Rare Books and Manuscripts.*

71 ▼
Charles Blunt [i.e., Blount]. **A Just Vindication of Learning and the Liberty of the Press.** London, 1695. *General Research.*

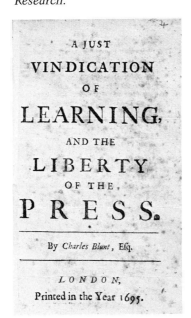

72
Blaise Pascal. **Les Provinciales: or, The Mysterie of Jesuitisme.** London, Printed by J. G. for R. Royston, 1657. *Rare Books and Manuscripts.*

73
Niccoló Machiavelli. **Il Prencipe.** [London, J. Wolfe] 1584. *Rare Books and Manuscripts.*

74 ▼
Cornelis Dusart. **Les heros de la Ligue.** Paris, Pere Peters, 1691. *Art, Prints and Photographs.*

75
Hubert Languet. **Vindiciae Contra Tyrannos.** Edinburgh, 1579. *Rare Books and Manuscripts.*

76
William Pynchon. **The Meritorious Price of Our Redemption.** London, Printed by J. M. for George Whittington, and James Moxon, 1650. *Rare Books and Manuscripts.*

77
William Prynne. **Histrio-Mastix. The Players Scourge; or, Actors Tragaedie.** London, Printed by E. A. and W. I. for Michael Sparke, 1633. *Rare Books and Manuscripts.*

78
John Eliot. **The Christian Commonwealth: or, The Civil Policy of the Rising Kingdom of Jesus Christ.** London, Printed for Livewell Chapman [1659]. *Rare Books and Manuscripts.*

79
Cyrano de Bergerac. **The Comical History of the States and Empires of the Worlds of the Moon and Sun.** London, Printed for Henry Rhodes, 1687. *Rare Books and Manuscripts.*

80
John Locke. **A Letter Concerning Toleration.** Boston, Printed and Sold by Rogers and Fowle, 1743. *Rare Books and Manuscripts.*

81
Ottavio Leoni. **Galileo Galilei.** 1624. Engraving. Image: 14.0 x 10.9 (5½ x 4⁵⁄₁₆). *Art, Prints and Photographs, Kennedy Fund.*

82
William Faithorne. **John Milton.** From Milton's *History of Britain,* 1670. Engraving. 18.1 x 13.5 (7⅛ x 5⁵⁄₁₆). *Art, Prints and Photographs, Beverly Chew bequest.*

83
Theodore Galle, after Jan van der Straet. **Title to *Nova Reperta* ["New Inventions"].** Ca. 1600. Engraving. 19.3 x 26.5 (7⅝ x 10⁷⁄₁₆). *Art, Prints and Photographs, Kennedy Fund.*

84
Theodore Galle, after Jan van der Straet. **Pulvis Pyrius ["Casting of Guns"].** From *Nova Reperta.* Ca. 1600. Engraving. 19.0 x 26.8 (7½ x 10⁹⁄₁₆). *Art, Prints and Photographs, Kennedy Fund.*

85

Theodore Galle, after Jan van der Straet.
Distillatio ["Distilling"]. From *Nova
Reperta.* Ca. 1600. Engraving. 19.0 x 26.9
(7⁷⁄₁₆ x 10⁹⁄₁₆). *Art, Prints and
Photographs, Kennedy Fund.*

86

Theodore Galle, after Jan van der Straet.
Impressio Librorum ["Printing Office"].
From *Nova Reperta.* Ca. 1600. Engraving.
18.7 x 26.6 (7³⁄₈ x 10½). *Art, Prints and
Photographs, Kennedy Fund.*

87

Hans Collaert, after Jan van der Straet.
Astrolabium ["The Astrolabe"]. From
Nova Reperta. Ca. 1600. Engraving.
18.6 x 27.2 (7⁵⁄₁₆ x 10¹¹⁄₁₆). *Art, Prints and
Photographs, Kennedy Fund.*

88 ▾

Theodore Galle, after Jan van der Straet.
Lapis Polaris, Magnes ["The Magnetic
North Pole"]. From *Nova Reperta.* Ca.
1600. Engraving. 19.1 x 27.0 (7½ x 10⅝).
*Art, Prints and Photographs, Kennedy
Fund.*

III
Free Expression
and Revolution,
1689–1800

89

Charles de Secondat de Montesquieu.
De l'Esprit des Loix. 2v. Geneva, Barillot &
fils, 1748. *Rare Books and Manuscripts.*

90 ▲

[Diderot Encyclopedia] **Encyclopédie,
ou Dictionnaire Raisonné des Sciences,
des Arts et des Métiers.** Vol. 1. Paris,
Briasson, et al., 1751. *General Research.*

91

Denis Diderot. **Pensées Philosophiques.**
[Paris?] Aux Indes, Chez Bedihuldgemale,
1748. *Lent by a Baltimore collector.*

92

Claude Adrien Helvétius. **De l'Esprit.**
Paris, Chez Durand, 1758. *General
Research.*

93

Jean-Jacques Rousseau. **Julie ou La
Nouvelle Héloïse. Lettres de deux amans.**
2v. London, 1774. *Art, Prints and
Photographs.*

94

Jean-Jacques Rousseau. **Emile, ou de
l'Education.** The Hague, Jean Néaulme,
1762. *Rare Books and Manuscripts.*

95

Jean-Jacques Rousseau. **A Treatise on the
Social Compact.** London, T. Becket and
P. A. De Hondt, 1764. *General Research.*

96

François Marie Arouet de Voltaire.
Letters Concerning the English Nation.
London, C. Davis and A. Lyon, 1733.
Rare Books and Manuscripts.

97

François Marie Arouet de Voltaire.
Candid: or, All for the Best. London,
J. Nourse, 1759. *Rare Books and
Manuscripts.*

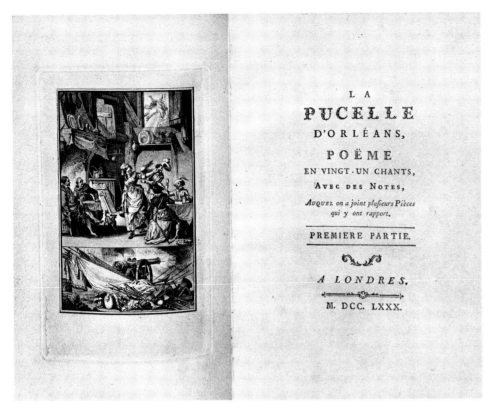

98 ▲
François Marie Arouet de Voltaire.
La Pucelle d'Orléans. London [i.e., Paris,
Cazin] 1780. *Spencer Collection.*

99
François Marie Arouet de Voltaire.
**Letters from M. de Voltaire. To Several of
His Friends. Translated from the French
by the Rev. Dr. Franklin.** Dublin, Printed
for H. Saunders, 1770. *Rare Books and
Manuscripts.*

100
Pierre Augustin Caron de Beaumarchais.
**La folle journée; ou, Le mariage de
Figaro.** [Paris?] 1785. *Music Division,
Drexel Collection.*

101 ▲
Immanuel Kant. **Die Religion innerhalb
der Grenzen der blossen Vernunft.**
Neuwied, 1793. *General Research.*

102
David Hume. **Essays and Treatises on
Several Subjects.** London, A. Millar, 1758.
*General Research. Presented by Roswell
Skeel, Jr., and Emily Ellsworth Ford
Skeel.*

103
John Locke. **An Essay Concerning The
True Original Extent and End of Civil
Government.** Boston, Edes and Gill, 1773.
Rare Books and Manuscripts.

104
Thomas Maule. **New-England
Pe[r]secutors Mauled with Their Own
Weapons.** [London, 1661] *Rare Books
and Manuscripts.*

105
New-York Gazette. Newspaper. 1734–35.
Rare Books and Manuscripts.

106
New-York Weekly Journal. Newspaper.
1734–35. *Rare Books and Manuscripts.*

107
**Remarks on the Trial of John-Peter
Zenger, printer of the New-York Weekly
Journal.** London, J. Roberts, 1738. *Rare
Books and Manuscripts.*

108
North Briton. Weekly. Nos. 1–46 (June 5,
1762–April 30, 1763). London. *Rare
Books and Manuscripts.*

109
John Wilkes. **The Conduct of the
Administration, in the Prosecution of
Mr. Wilkes.** London, J. Wilkie, 1764.
Rare Books and Manuscripts.

110
Extraordinary North Briton. Weekly. Nos.
35–90 (January 7, 1769–January 27, 1770)
London. *Rare Books and Manuscripts.*

111
**Communication from Committee of
Correspondence of Abington** in the
Massachusetts Bay Colony to the
Committee of Correspondence at Boston.
April 27, 1773. *Rare Books and
Manuscripts.*

112
**Communication from Committee of
Correspondence of Abington** in the
Massachusetts Bay Colony to Committee
of Correspondence at Boston. July 29,
1773. *Rare Books and Manuscripts.*

113
**Complaint of Chairman of the
Committee of Correspondence to "one
of the Justices assigned to keep the Peace**
within and for the County of Suffolk"
in Massachusetts that one Nathaniel
Barber "in his private discourse and
conversation" is discouraging citizens
from supporting the Declaration of
Independence. April 8, 1777. *Rare Books
and Manuscripts.*

114
**Letter from the Chairman of the
Committee of Correspondence at Boston
to John Hancock** as "Governour in
and over said Commonwealth of
Massachusetts" urging measures be
taken to protect citizens against "Letters
& Packages" arriving on ships. November
10, 1780. *Rare Books and Manuscripts.*

115
Boston Chronicle. Newspaper. 1769.
Rare Books and Manuscripts.

116
Massachusetts Spy. Newspaper. Vol. 5,
no. 219 (May 3, 1775). Worcester, Mass.,
Isaiah Thomas, printer. *Rare Books and
Manuscripts.*

117
Thomas Paine. **Common Sense;
Addressed to the Inhabitants of America.**
Philadelphia, R. Bell, 1776. *Rare Books
and Manuscripts.*

118
Thomas Jefferson. **Draft of the
Declaration of Independence.** 1776.
Rare Books and Manuscripts.

119
Edmund Burke. **A Letter.** London,
J. Dodsley, 1777. *Rare Books and
Manuscripts.*

120
Guillaume Thomas François Raynal.
Histoire Philosophique et Politique. 7v.
Amsterdam, 1773–74. *Rare Books and
Manuscripts.*

121
France. Conseil d'Etat. **Arrest du Conseil
d'Etat du Roi, qui Supprime un Imprimé
Ayant pour Titre: Histoire Philosophique
& Politique des Etablissements & du
Commerce dans les Deux Indes. Du 19
Décembre 1772.** [Paris, Chez P. G. Simon,
Imprimeur du Parlement, 1773] *Rare
Books and Manuscripts.*

122
Guy Jean Baptiste Target. **La Censure.**
[Paris?] 1775. *General Research.*

123
Communauté des Libraires et
Imprimeurs de Paris. **Code de la Librairie
et Imprimerie de Paris.** Paris, 1744.
General Research.

124
Guillaume Imbert. **La Chronique
Scandaleuse.** 2v. Paris, 1785. *General
Research.*

125
Charles Thévenot de Morande. **Le
Gazetier Cuirassé : ou Anecdotes
Scandaleuses de la Cour de France.**
London, 1771. *General Research.*

126
Le Chevalier Fr. N. **Les Memoirs
authentiques de la Comtesse de Barrée.**
London, 1772. *General Research.*

127
**Gravures Historiques des Principaux
Evénements depuis l'Ouverture des Etats
Généraux de 1789.** Paris, Chez Janinet &
Cussac, 1789. *Art, Prints and
Photographs.*

128
**Lettre à un Censeur Royal, sur la Liberté
de la Presse.** [Paris, Volland, 1789?]
General Research.

129
Révolutions de Paris. 1–13 (1789). Paris.
General Research.

130
France. Constitution. **Constitution de la
République Française, Proposée au Peuple
Français par la Convention Nationale.**
Includes **Declaration of the Rights of
Man and Citizen.** Paris, De l'Imprimerie de
la République, 1795. *General Research.*

131
Edmund Burke. **Reflections on the
Revolution in France.** London, J. Dodsley,
1790. *General Research.*

132
Thomas Paine. **Rights of Man, Being an
Answer to Mr. Burke's Attack on the
French Revolution.** London, J. S. Jordan,
1791. *Rare Books and Manuscripts.*

133
Thomas Paine. **Rights of Man. Part
the Second, Combining Principle and
Practice.** Boston, Thomas and John Fleet,
1792. *Rare Books and Manuscripts.*

134
Mary Wollstonecraft Godwin. **A
Vindication of the Rights of Woman.**
London, J. Johnson, 1792. *Rare Books and
Manuscripts.*

135
Thomas Paine. **Recueil des Divers Ecrits.**
Paris, F. Buisson, 1793. *Rare Books and
Manuscripts.*

136
Thomas Paine. **The Trial of Thomas
Paine, for Certain False, Wicked,
Scandalous, and Seditious Libels Inserted
in the Second Part of the Rights of Man.**
London [1792]. *Rare Books and
Manuscripts.*

137
James Lyon. **The Scourge of Aristocracy.**
October–December, 1798. Fairhaven, Vt.,
1798. *Rare Books and Manuscripts.*

138
John Thomson. **An Enquiry, Concerning
the Liberty, and Licentiousness of the
Press.** New York, Johnson & Stryker,
1801. *General Research.*

139
Tunis Wortman. **A Treatise Concerning
Political Enquiry, and the Liberty of the
Press.** New York, Printed by G. Forman
for the author, 1800. *Rare Books and
Manuscripts.*

140
Jean Huber. **Voltaire Portrait Studies.**
Ca. 1777. Etching. Image: 30.4 x 27.7
(11¹¹⁄₁₆ x 10⅞). *Art, Prints and
Photographs, Norrie Fund.*

141
William Hogarth. **John Wilkes Esqr.** 1763.
Engraving. 35.6 x 23.0 (14 x 9¹⁄₁₆). *Art,
Prints and Photographs, Samuel J. Tilden
bequest.*

142 ▲
Anonymous British. **The Repeal** [of the
Stamp Act]. 1766. Etching. Image:
27.4 x 44.7 (10¹³⁄₁₆ x 17⁹⁄₁₆). *Art, Prints
and Photographs, Samuel J. Tilden
bequest.*

143
Anonymous British. **Poor Old England
Endeavoring to Reclaim His Wicked
American Children.** 1777. Etching.
20.2 x 32.7 (8 x 12⅞). *Art, Prints and
Photographs, gift of Mrs. J. Percy Sabin.*

144
Anonymous British. **The Horse America, Throwing His Master.** 1779. Colored etching. Image: 17.2 x 27.6 (6¾ x 10⅞). *Art, Prints and Photographs, gift of Mrs. J. Percy Sabin.*

145
James Gillray. **A Family of Sans Culotts Refreshing after the Fatigues of the Day.** 1792. Etching. 25.2 x 35.4 (9¹⁵⁄₁₆ x 13¹⁵⁄₁₆). *Art, Prints and Photographs, Samuel J. Tilden Bequest.*

146
James Gillray. **The Zenith of French Glory.** 1793. Colored etching. 35.5 x 25.0 (13¹⁵⁄₁₆ x 9¹³⁄₁₆). *Art, Prints and Photographs, Samuel J. Tilden bequest.*

147
James Gillray. **The Rights of Man.** 1791. Colored etching. 35.4 x 25.1 (13¹⁵⁄₁₆ x 9⅞). *Art, Prints and Photographs, Samuel J. Tilden bequest.*

148
James Gillray. **Tom Paine's Nightly Pest.** 1792. Colored etching. Image: 29.1 x 36 (11⁷⁄₁₆ x 14³⁄₁₆). *Art, Prints and Photographs, Samuel J. Tilden bequest.*

IV
The Emergence of Moral Censorship, 1800–1890

149
John Stuart Mill. **On Liberty.** London, J. W. Parker and Son, 1859. *General Research.*

150
Alexis de Tocqueville. **Democracy in America. Part the Second, the Social Influence of Democracy.** New York, J. & H. G. Langley, 1840. *Rare Books and Manuscripts, Stuart Collection.*

151
Johann Gottlieb Fichte. **Reden an die deutsche Nation.** Leipzig, Friedrich Ludwig Herbig, 1824. *General Research.*

152 ▲
Heinrich Heine. **Buch der Lieder.** Hamburg, Hoffmann und Campe, 1827. *Rare Books and Manuscripts.*

153
Johann Wolfgang von Goethe. **Egmont.** Leipzig, G. J. Göschen, 1788. *General Research.*

154
Giuseppe Mazzini. **L'Italie, l'Autriche et le Pape.** Paris, Imp. Schneider et Langrand, 1845. *General Research.*

155
Johann Joseph von Goerres. **Teutschland und die Revolution.** Teutschland [Coblenz], 1819. *General Research.*

156
Jean-Ignace Isidor Gérard, called Grandville, and Eugène Forest. **Résurrection de la censure.** From *La Caricature*, January 5, 1832. Lithograph. 21.8 x 26.6 (8⅝ x 10½). *Art, Prints and Photographs, John Shaw Billings Memorial Fund.*

157
Charles Philipon. **Projet d'un monument Expia-poire à éleves sur la place de la révolution, précisément à la place oú fut guillotiné Louis XVI.** From *La Caricature*, June 7, 1832. Lithograph. 21.0 x 29.5 (8⁵⁄₁₆ x 11⅝). *Art, Prints and Photographs, John Shaw Billings Memorial Fund.*

158
Auguste Desperet with Jean-Ignace Isidor Gérard, called Grandville. **O soleil de Juillet, viens vite.** From *La Caricature*, April 9, 1835. Lithograph. 20.6 x 28.6 (8⅛ x 11¼). *Art, Prints and Photographs, John Shaw Billings Memorial Fund.*

159
Auguste Bouquet. **La Poire et ses pépins.** From *La Caricature*, July 4, 1833. Lithograph. 34.9 x 29.6 (13¾ x 11¹¹⁄₁₆). *Art, Prints and Photographs, John Shaw Billings Memorial Fund.*

160
The Liberator. Newspaper. Boston. Vol. 5, no. 33 (August 15, 1835). *General Research.*

161
Alton Trials. New York, John F. Trow, 1838. *General Research.*

162
Elijah P. Lovejoy. **Memoir of the Rev. Elijah P. Lovejoy; Who Was Murdered in Defence of the Liberty of the Press, at Alton, Illinois, Nov. 7, 1837.** New York, John S. Taylor, 1838. *General Research.*

163 ▼
Harriet Beecher Stowe. **Uncle Tom's Cabin; or, Life Among the Lowly.** 2v. Boston, John P. Jewett & Co., 1852. *General Research.*

LITTLE EVA READING THE BIBLE TO UNCLE TOM IN THE ARBOR. Page 68

164
Harriet Beecher Stowe. **Uncle Tom's Cabin.** Manuscript portion of first draft of first chapter. [Undated] *Rare Books and Manuscripts.*

165
Richard H. Colfax. **Evidence Against the Views of the Abolitionists, Consisting of Physical and Moral Proofs, of the Natural Inferiority of the Negroes.** New York, J. T. M. Bleakley, 1833. *Schomburg Collection.*

166
George Fitzhugh. **Cannibals All! or, Slaves Without Masters.** Richmond, Va., A. Morris, 1857. *Schomburg Collection.*

167
Frederick Douglass. **Narrative of the Life of Frederick Douglass, an American Slave. Written by Himself.** Boston, Pub. at the Anti-Slavery Office, 1845. *General Research.*

168
Theodore Dwight Weld. **The Bible Against Slavery.** New York, American Anti-Slavery Society, 1838. *General Research.*

169
Charles Darwin. **On the Origin of Species by Means of Natural Selection.** London, John Murray, 1859. *Rare Books and Manuscripts.*

170
Society for the Suppression of Vice. Brief Abstract of Their Proceedings, During the First Year of Their Establishment. [London, 1803] *General Research.*

171
Mason Locke Weems. **The Drunkard's Looking-Glass.** [Philadelphia] 1813. *Rare Books and Manuscripts.*

172
Hannah More. **Christian Morals.** New York, Richard Scott, 1813. *General Research.*

173
William Shakespeare. **Works. The Family Shakspeare.** Edited by Thomas Bowdler. 10v. London, Longman et al., 1818. *General Research.*

174
Francis Beaumont. **Beaumont and Fletcher; or, the Finest Scenes, and Other Beauties of Those Two Poets, now First Selected from the Whole of Their Works, to the Exclusion of Whatever Is Morally Objectionable....** London, H. G. Bohn, 1855. *Lent by David H. Stam.*

175 ▲
Elizabeth Cleghorn Stevenson Gaskell. **Cranford.** London, Macmillan, 1892. *Lent by Martha Driver.*

176
William Makepeace Thackeray. **Autograph letter signed to Elizabeth Barrett Browning** rejecting her poem *Lord Walter's Wife.* [London] April 2, 1861. *Berg Collection.*

177
William Makepeace Thackeray. **Vanity Fair.** London, Bradbury and Evans, 1848. *Rare Books and Manuscripts.*

178
Gustave Flaubert. **Madame Bovary.** 2v. New York, Printed for Subscribers by George H. Richmond & Co. [1896]. *General Research.*

179 ▼
Anthony Comstock. **Traps for the Young.** New York, Funk & Wagnalls Co. [1883]. *General Research.*

180
Théophile Gautier. **Mademoiselle de Maupin.** Paris, Charpentier, 1866. *General Research.*

181
François Rabelais. **The Works of Rabelais Faithfully Translated from the French.** London, J. C. Hotten [1871]. *General Research.*

182
Charles Knowlton. **Fruits of Philosophy: or the Private Companion of Adult People.** Philadelphia, F. P. Rogers, 1839. *Lent by the New York Academy of Medicine.*

183
John Cleland. **Memoirs of Fanny Hill.** Paris, Isidore Liseux, 1888. *General Research.*

184
Nathaniel Hawthorne. **The Scarlet Letter.** Boston, Ticknor et al., 1850. *Rare Books and Manuscripts.*

185
Samuel L. Clemens. **Adventures of Huckleberry Finn.** New York, Charles L. Webster and Co., 1885. *Rare Books and Manuscripts.*

186
Walt Whitman. **Leaves of Grass. [Blue Book]** Boston, Thayer and Eldridge, 1860–61. Whitman's own copy, with his annotations and corrections. *Rare Books and Manuscripts.*

187
Walt Whitman. **Leaves of Grass.** Boston, J. R. Osgood, 1881–82. *Rare Books and Manuscripts.*

188
Honoré Daumier. **Ah! tu veux te frotter à la presse!!** ["Ah! You want to step on the press!!"]. From *La Caricature,* no. 152, October 3, 1833. Lithograph. 23.0 x 20.8 (9¹/₁₆ x 8³/₁₆). *Art, Prints and Photographs, C.J. Lawrence Collection.*

189
Honoré Daumier. **Liberté de la press. Ne vous y frottez pas!!** ["Liberty of the press. Don't meddle with it!!"]. From *L' Association mensuelle,* March 1834. Lithograph. 32.5 x 45.0 (12¹³/₁₆ x 17¹¹/₁₆). *Art, Prints and Photographs, S.P. Avery Collection.*

190
Honoré Daumier. **Baisser le rideau, la farce est jouée** ["Lower the curtain, the farce is played"]. From *La Caricature,* no. 201, September 11, 1834. Lithograph. 20.0 x 27.8 (7⁷/₈ x 10¹⁵/₁₆). *Art, Prints and Photographs, C.J. Lawrence Collection.*

191
Dalziel Brothers, after John Dawson Watson. **Illustration to "a Summer's Eve in a Country Lane."** From *London Society Magazine,* August 1862. Wood engraving. 19.0 x 11.7 (7½ x 4⁵/₈). *Art, Prints and Photographs.*

192
Dalziel Brothers, after John Dawson Watson. **Illustration to "Married! Married! And Not to Me."** From *London Society Magazine,* November 1862. Wood engraving. 9.6 x 7.7 (3¾ x 3). *Art, Prints and Photographs.*

193
Dalziel Brothers, after Arthur Boyd Houghton. **My Treasure.** From *Touches of Nature,* 1861. Wood engraving. 16.5 x 12.0 (6⁷/₁₆ x 4¾). *Art, Prints and Photographs.*

194
After Charles Samuel Keene. **Embarrassing.** From *Punch,* June 19, 1869. Wood engraving. 11.4 x 9.3 (4½ x 3¾). *Art, Prints and Photographs.*

195
Joseph Swain, after Matthew James Lawless. **Illustration to "The Head Master's Sister."** From *Once a Week,* April 28, 1860. Wood engraving. 10.0 x 12.7 (3¹⁵/₁₆ x 5). *Art, Prints and Photographs.*

196
After George Du Maurier. **Distressing Dilemma for Our Young Bachelor Surgeon!** From *Punch,* December 16, 1865. Wood engraving. 11.4 x 17.4 (4½ x 6¹³/₁₆). *Art, Prints and Photographs.*

197 ▼
William Finden, after David Wilkie. **The Highlander's Return.** 1845. Engraving. 51.0 x 67.5 (20¹/₁₆ x 26⁹/₁₆). *Art, Prints and Photographs.*

198
Edouard Manet. **The Execution of the Emperor Maximilian.** 1867; printed 1884. Lithograph. 33.3 x 43.3 (13¹/₁₆ x 17¹/₁₆). *Art, Prints and Photographs, S.P. Avery Collection.*

199
Edouard Manet. **Polichinelle.** 1874; printed 1876. Color lithograph. 42.9 x 31.3 (16⁷/₈ x 12³/₈). *Art, Prints and Photographs, S.P. Avery Collection.*

200
Francisco José de Goya y Lucientes. **Y no hai remedio** ["And there's no help for it"]. From *The Disasters of War.* 1810–20; first published, 1863. Etching and lavis. 14.1 x 16.8 (5⁹/₁₆ x 6⁵/₈). *Art, Prints and Photographs, S.P. Avery Collection.*

201
Francisco José de Goya y Lucientes. **Se aprovechan** ["They make use of them"]. From *The Disasters of War.* 1810–20; first published, 1863. Etching and lavis. 15.9 x 23.5 (6¼ x 9¼). *Art, Prints and Photographs, S.P. Avery Collection.*

202
Francisco José de Goya y Lucientes. **Nada. Ello dirá.** ["Nothing. The Event Will Tell."]. From *The Disasters of War.* 1810–20; first published 1863. Etching, aquatint and lavis. 15.3 x 20.0 (6 x 7⁷/₈). *Art, Prints and Photographs, S.P. Avery Collection.*

203
Stephen Crane. **Maggie, a Girl of the Streets.** New York, D. Appleton and Company, 1896. *Rare Books and Manuscripts.*

204
Theodore Dreiser. **Sister Carrie.** Manuscript. Vol. 1. 1900. *Rare Books and Manuscripts.*

205
Theodore Dreiser. **The "Genius."** New York, London, J. Lane, 1915. *Berg Collection.*

206
Authors' League of America. **[Protest (typewritten copy) against the suppression of Theodore Dreiser's *The Genius*]** 1916. *Berg Collection.*

207
Letter of Theodore Dreiser to H. L. Mencken stating that *Harper's* had decided not to publish **The Titan,** even though 10,000 copies had been printed. March 6, 1914. Autograph letter signed. *Rare Books and Manuscripts.*

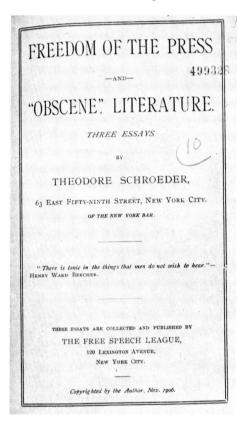

208 ▲
Theodore Schroeder. **Freedom of the Press and "Obscene" Literature.** New York, The Free Speech League, ca. 1906. *General Research.*

209
Edwin C. Walker. **Who Is the Enemy; Anthony Comstock, or You?** New York, Published by Edwin C. Walker, 1903. *General Research.*

210
Robert Minor. **"Your Honor, This Woman Gave Birth to a Naked Child."** [*The Masses.* Vol. 6, no. 12 (September 1915)] *Lent by Tamiment Archives/New York University.*

211
Robert Dale Owen. **Moral Physiology.** New York, G. W. & A. J. Matsell, 1835. *General Research.*

212
Francis Place. **Illustrations and Proofs of the Principle of Population.** London, Printed for Longman, Hurst, Rees, Orme, and Brown, 1822. *Economic and Public Affairs.*

213
Margaret H. Sanger. **What Every Girl Should Know.** [New York, M. N. Maisel, 1920] *Lent by Margaret Sanger Center/ Planned Parenthood of New York.*

214
Margaret H. Sanger. **Family Limitation.** [New York? 191—?] *Lent by Margaret Sanger Center/Planned Parenthood of New York.*

215
The Woman Rebel. New York. Vol. 1, no. 7 (September–October 1914). *Lent by Margaret Sanger Center/Planned Parenthood of New York.*

216
Photograph of Margaret Sanger among group of supporters. *Lent by Margaret Sanger Center/Planned Parenthood of New York.*

217
Photograph showing waiting room of the Sanger Clinic. *Lent by Margaret Sanger Center/Planned Parenthood of New York.*

218
Photograph showing arrest of Margaret Sanger. *Lent by Margaret Sanger Center/ Planned Parenthood of New York.*

219
Theodore Schroeder. **Our Vanishing Liberty of the Press.** New York, Free Speech League, 1906. *General Research.*

220
Mother Earth; Monthly Magazine Devoted to Social Science and Literature. Vol. 7, no. 10 (December 1912). New York. *General Research.*

221
Industrial Workers of the World. **One Big Union of the I.W.W.** Chicago, Ill., Industrial Workers of the World [191—?]. *General Research.*

222
Letter of Jack London to his agent expressing his concern that *The People of the Abyss* is too "radical" for publication by the "orthodox magazines" in the United States. January 30, 1903. *Rare Books and Manuscripts.*

223
Letter of Jack London to his agent with mention of changes he has made in *The People of the Abyss* in the hope that it might be published in the United States. February 16, 1903. Typed letter signed. *Rare Books and Manuscripts.*

224
Letter of Stella Ballantine to Frank Walsh asking his help in behalf of Emma Goldman, whose mail was not being delivered to her while in federal prison. March 25, 1918. Typed letter signed. *Rare Books and Manuscripts.*

225
Copy of letter of Frank Walsh to Stella Ballantine detailing his efforts in behalf of Emma Goldman. March 21, 1918. *Rare Books and Manuscripts.*

226
Letter from George Creel, Chairman of the Committee on Public Information, to Ralph M. Easley of the League for National Unity giving his view that the Senate investigation of the German American Alliance had led to its dissolution. June 27, 1918. Typed letter signed. *Rare Books and Manuscripts.*

227
Envelope, labeled "Opened by Censor," received by John Quinn on April 19, 1918. *Rare Books and Manuscripts.*

228
Boardman Robinson. **"All Ready to Fight for Liberty."** [*The Masses.* Vol. 9, no. 8 (June 1917)] *Lent by Tamiment Archives/ New York University.*

229
Letter of Amos Pinchot to Woodrow Wilson protesting the trial for conspiracy of Max Eastman, Art Young, and John Reed of *The Masses* for views on the war and conscription which had been aired in that publication. May 24, 1918. Typed letter signed. *Rare Books and Manuscripts.*

230
Harrison George. **Is Freedom Dead?** Chicago, I.W.W. Publishing Bureau [1918]. *General Research.*

231
Thomas Everett Harré. **The I.W.W.** [New York] 1918. *General Research.*

232
Karl Marx. **Das Kapital.** Hamburg, Verlag von Otto Meissner, 1867. *General Research.*

233
Karl Marx and Friedrich Engels. **Manifesto of the Communist Party.** New York, New York Labor News Company, 1888. *Rare Books and Manuscripts.*

234 ▲
Emil Nolde. **Conversation.** 1917. Woodcut. 12.3 x 16.0 (4¹³⁄₁₆ x 6¼). *Art, Prints and Photographs, Kennedy Fund.*

235
Emil Nolde. **Young Couple.** 1917. Woodcut. 32.3 x 23.9 (12¹¹⁄₁₆ x 9⅜). *Art, Prints and Photographs, Weitenkampf Fund.*

236
Max Beckmann. **Adam and Eve.** 1917. Etching. 23.8 x 17.7 (9⅜ x 6¹⁵⁄₁₆). *Art, Prints and Photographs, Norrie Fund.*

237
Félicien Rops. **The Abduction.** From *The Satanics.* Ca. 1886. Heliogravure, soft-ground and burnishing. 24.1 x 21.1 (11⅛ x 8⁵⁄₁₆). *Art, Prints and Photographs, Kennedy Fund.*

238
Théophile Alexandre Steinlen. **18 March.** 1894. Stencil colored lithograph. 36.0 x 32.0 (14³⁄₁₆ x 12⁹⁄₁₆). *Art, Prints and Photographs, Norrie Fund.*

239
Théophile Alexandre Steinlen. **The New Year.** 1893. Stencil colored lithograph. 32.6 x 28.6 (12¹³⁄₁₆ x 11¼). *Art, Prints and Photographs, Norrie Fund.*

240
Théophile Alexandre Steinlen. **The Cry of the Streets.** 1894. Stencil colored lithograph. 32.4 x 29.4 (12¾ x 11½). *Art, Prints and Photographs, Norrie Fund.*

241
Kasimir Severinovich Malevich. **"What a Boom! What a Blast There Was from the Germans at Lomza!"** 1915. Color lithograph. 33.3 x 51.0 (13¼ x 20¼). *Art, Prints and Photographs, Kennedy Fund.*

242
Kasimir Severinovich Malevich. **Wilhelm's Merry-Go-Round. "On the Outskirts of Paris My Army Is Being Beaten Up. I'm Just Running Around and Can't Do a Thing."** 1914–15. Color lithograph. 33.3 x 52.3 (13¼ x 20⁹⁄₁₆). *Art, Prints and Photographs, Kennedy Fund.*

243
Kasimir Severinovich Malevich. **"An Austrian Went to Radziwill and Came Right on to a Peasant Woman's Pitchfork."** 1914–15. Color lithograph. 33.0 x 49.3 (13 x 19⁷⁄₁₆). *Art, Prints and Photographs, Kennedy Fund.*

244
Art Young. **Taking his measure.** **"Capitalist: 'Poor? Why man you are getting fat.' Capitalist Legislator: 'Sure you are—why I've just written a speech to prove it.' "** For *Life.* 1911. Pen drawing. 33.4 x 40.5 (13³⁄₁₆ x 15¹¹⁄₁₆). *Art, Prints and Photographs, gift of the artist.*

245
Art Young. **The Hand That Rocks the Cradle.** For *Life.* Date unknown. Pendrawing. 25.6 x 36.8 (10¹⁄₁₆ x 14½). *Art, Prints and Photographs, gift of the artist.*

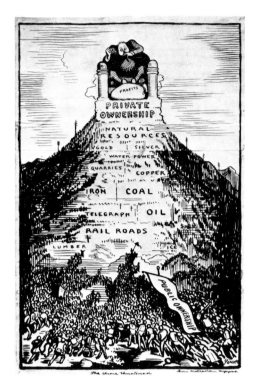

246 ▲
Art Young. **The Throne Threatened.** For
The Metropolitan Magazine. Between
1912 and 1917. Pen drawing. 32.9 x 21.8
(12¹⁵⁄₁₆ x 8⁹⁄₁₆). *Art, Prints and
Photographs, gift of the artist.*

247 ▲
James Branch Cabell. **Jurgen.** London,
John Lane, 1921. *General Research.*

248
**Letter of James Branch Cabell to H. L.
Mencken.** Typed letter signed. January
21, 1920. *Rare Books and Manuscripts.*

249
Letter of B. W. Huebsch to John Quinn.
Typed letter signed. April 5, 1921. *Rare
Books and Manuscripts.*

250
The Little Review. Broadside announcing
final issue. Undated. Mitchell Kennerly
Papers/Margaret Anderson File. *Rare
Books and Manuscripts.*

251
The Little Review. Vol. 7, no. 2 (July/
August 1920). New York. *Berg Collection.*

252
Letter to John Quinn from "AE" [i.e.,
George William Russell]. Autograph
letter signed. January 1, 1921. *Rare Books
and Manuscripts.*

253
Radclyffe Hall. **The Well of Loneliness.**
New York, Covici-Friede Publishers,
1928. *General Research.*

254
David Herbert Lawrence. **Lady
Chatterley's Lover.** Florence, privately
printed, 1928. *Lent by Katherine B.
Crum.*

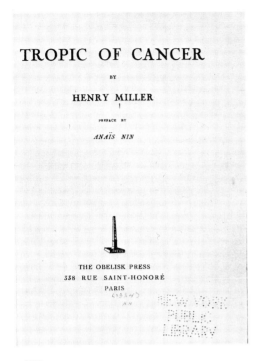

255 ▲
Henry Miller. **Tropic of Cancer.** Paris, The Obelisk Press [1934]. *Rare Books and Manuscripts.*

256
Jean Genêt. **Querelle de Brest.** [Paris, 1947] *Spencer Collection.*

257
Allen Ginsberg. **Howl, and Other Poems.** San Francisco, City Lights Books, 1956. *Lent by Arthur Strange.*

258
William Burroughs. **The Naked Lunch.** Paris, Olympia Press, 1959. *General Research.*

259
[Scopes Trial] **The World's Most Famous Court Trial: Tennessee Evolution Case.** Cincinnati, Ohio, National Book Co. [ca. 1925]. *General Research.*

260
Chattanooga Daily Times. Newspaper. July 14, 1925. *General Research.*

261
Truman J. Moon. **Biology for Beginners.** New York, et al., Holt, Rinehart and Winston, 1981. Facsimile of 1921 edition. *Lent by Holt, Rinehart and Winston.*

262
Statements regarding the use of the Rugg Series of social science texts in the Englewood school system. Compiled by a committee of parents and taxpayers. Englewood, N. J., 1940. *General Research.*

263
Walter Gropius. **The New Architecture and the Bauhaus.** London, Faber and Faber Limited, 1935. *Art, Prints and Photographs.*

264
Sigmund Freud. **Das Unbehagen in der Kultur.** Vienna, Internationaler Psychoanalytischer Verlag, 1930. *General Research.*

265
Schalom Asch. **Die Mutter.** Zurich, Paul Zsolnay Verlag, 1930. *Jewish Division.*

266
Eduard Beneš. **Democracy Today and Tomorrow.** New York, Macmillan Company, 1939. *General Research.*

267
Charles de Gaulle. **The Army of the Future.** Philadelphia and New York, J. B. Lippincott Company, 1941. *General Research.*

268
Franz Werfel. **Das Lied von Bernadette.** Stockholm, Bermann-Fischer Verlag, 1941. *General Research.*

269
Arnold Zweig. **The Case of Sergeant Grischa.** London, Martin Secker, 1928. *General Research.*

270
André Gide. **The Vatican Swindle (Les Caves du Vatican).** New York, Alfred A. Knopf, 1925. *General Research.*

271
Siegfried Kracauer. **Soziologie als Wissenschaft.** Dresden, Sibyllen-Verlag, 1922. *General Research.*

272
Léon Blum. **La Réforme Gouvernementale.** Paris, Editions Bernard Grasset, 1936. *General Research.*

273
Karl Kautsky. **Die proletarische Revolution und ihr Programm.** Stuttgart and Berlin, J. W. H. Dietz Nachfolger, 1922. *General Research.*

274
The Communist International. Vol. 9, no. 6 (April 1, 1932). New York. *General Research.*

275
American Civil Liberties Union. **Eternal Vigilance! The Story of Civil Liberty, 1937–1938.** New York, American Civil Liberties Union, 1938. *General Research.*

276
George Orwell. **Nineteen Eighty-Four.** London, Secker & Warburg, 1949. *Berg Collection.*

277
Anonymous Russian. **Monastery Life.** Kharkov, Ukrainian Soviet Socialist Republic, Path of Enlightenment, 1923. Poster. 50.8 x 69.8 (20 x 27½). *Lent by Todd Bludeau.*

278
Anonymous Russian. **The October Revolution Is a Fight Against the Church and Religion for the Freedom of the Intellect and Science.** Kharkov, Ukrainian Soviet Socialist Republic, Path of Enlightenment, 1923. Poster. 50.8 x 69.8 (20 x 27½). *Lent by Todd Bludeau.*

279
Anonymous Russian. **Inquisition.** Kharkov, Ukrainian Soviet Socialist Republic, Path of Enlightenment, 1923. Poster. 69.8 x 50.8 (27½ x 20). *Lent by Todd Bludeau.*

280 ▲
Anonymous Russian. **Traffic in Church Rites.** Kharkov, Ukrainian Soviet Socialist Republic, Path of Enlightenment, 1923. Poster. 69.8 x 50.8 (27½ x 20). *Lent by Todd Bludeau.*

281
George Grosz. **"Under my rule it shall be brought to pass, that potatoes and small-bear shall be considered a holiday treat; and woe to him who meets my eye with the audacious front of health. Haggard want, and crouching fear, are my insignia; and in this livery will I clothe ye."** From *The Robbers.* 1920–21; published 1922. Lithograph. 48.1 x 37.6 (18¹⁵⁄₁₆ x 14¹³⁄₁₆). *Art, Prints and Photographs, Weitenkampf Fund.*

282
George Grosz. **"They thunder forth from their clouds about gentleness and forbearance, while they sacrifice human victims to the God of love."** From *The Robbers.* 1921–22; published 1922. Lithograph. 57.9 x 39.3 (22¹³⁄₁₆ x 15⁷⁄₁₆). *Art, Prints and Photographs, Friends of the Print Room.*

283
George Grosz. **"Poor hare! Thou playest but a sorry part in this world's drama, but your worshipful lords must needs have hares!"** From *The Robbers.* 1922. Photo lithograph. 48.5 x 39.2 (19⅛ x 12¹¹⁄₁₆). *Art, Prints and Photographs, Weitenkampf Fund.*

284
Vito Acconci. **3 Flags for 1 Space & 6 Regions.** 1981. Color photoetching and aquatint on six sheets. Total image: 130.9 x 157.5 (51½ x 62). *Art, Prints and Photographs, Kennedy Fund.*

285
Claes Oldenberg. **Proposal for a Monument to the Survival of the University of El Salvador: Blasted Pencil (Which Still Writes).** 1984. Color etching. Done for Artists Call against U.S. Intervention in Central America. *Art, Prints and Photographs, Kennedy Fund.*